Th...
from
Isaiah

WITHDRAWN

Ronald Youngblood

Regal
Books

A Division of GL Publications
Ventura, CA U.S.A

The translation of all Regal books is under the direction of GLINT. GLINT provides technical help for the adaptation, translation and publishing of books for millions of people worldwide. For information regarding translation, contact: GLINT, P.O. Box 6688, Ventura, California 93006.

Published by Regal Books
A Division of GL Publications
Ventura, California 93006
Printed in U.S.A.

Library of Congress Cataloging in Publication data

Youngblood, Ronald F.
    Themes from Isaiah.

    (A Bible commentary for laymen)
    Bibliography: p.
    1. Bible. O.T. Isaiah—Criticism, interpretation, etc.
I. Title.   II. Series.
BS1515.2.Y63   1984   224'.106   83-19128
ISBN 0-8307-0906-1

CONTENTS

PREFACE

Praise the LORD, O my soul;
   all my inmost being, praise his holy
name.
Praise the LORD, O my soul,
   and forget not all his benefits.
He forgives all my sins
   and heals all my diseases;
he redeems my life from the pit
   and crowns me with love and compassion.
He satisfies my desires with good things,
   so that my youth is renewed like the
eagle's.

These five verses, found at the beginning of Psalm 103, kept invading my consciousness as I was writing this book. Isaiah is in many respects a hymn of praise to God, who is good, and great, and gracious. The prophet lived in a turbulent period of Judah's history, but he never ceased to give praise to the Lord in spite of everything. Like the psalmist, Isaiah experienced forgiveness and healing, love and compassion, redemption and renewal. It is my fond prayer that you will sense God's presence in just as clear a way during your study of Isaiah's great prophecy.

The present commentary is divided into thirteen chapters for convenient use over the course of a quarter. After an introductory chapter, we treat the entire book of Isaiah section by section. Chapters 2—4 can be grouped together under the larger topic of "Isaiah's Ministry," 5—9 as "Isaiah's Internationalism," and 10—13 as "Isaiah's God."

The notes at the end of a few chapters and the selected bibliography at the end of the book are just a meager sampling of the extensive resources available for further study of the prophecy of Isaiah. My thanks are due to the host of commentators and students who have preceded me, to the publishers of Regal Books for their continued confidence in me, to my wife Carolyn and my children Glenn and Wendy for teaching me what it means to be a servant, and to Isaiah's God and mine for strengthening me in my weakness and forgiving me in spite of my disobedience.

Ronald Youngblood

1

ISAIAH

An Introduction

The book of Isaiah is universally recognized as the greatest prophetic book in the Old Testament. It is not the longest of the prophetic books (that honor goes to Jeremiah, which is 20 percent longer than Isaiah and is the longest book in the entire Old Testament, containing a larger number of words than any other Old Testament book). It does not have more chapters than any other book in the Old Testament (that honor goes to the Psalms). It does not have more verses than any other Old Testament book (the Psalms wins in that category also).

What is it, then, that makes Isaiah such a remarkable book?

The measure of any book's greatness is not to be looked for in the quantity of its lines or paragraphs or pages but in the quality of its contents. The book of Isaiah is great because of the breadth of its teachings, because of the importance of its message, because of the sweep of its subject matter. The Colorado River has many gorges, but none is so magnificent as the Grand Canyon: 280 miles long, 4 to 18 miles wide and over a mile deep, it beckons to the visitor to marvel at its beauty and plumb its depths again and again. In much the same way the Old Testament has many prophetic books, but none is so magnificent as Isaiah: sixty-six chapters long and thus a miniature Bible in itself, it beckons to the reader to revel in its beauty and plumb its teachings again and again.

Although God Himself is the ultimate Author of the book of Isaiah, He caused its inspired words to be written down by one of His choicest servants. A man named Isaiah produced a book called Isaiah, and the latter bears the unmistakable imprint of the former's life and times.

THE MAN

Himself

By any standard one might wish to use, the prophet Isaiah was one of the greatest theologians of all time. He knew God intimately and obeyed Him faithfully; he understood God's will clearly and proclaimed it fearlessly. He was a prince, a patriot, a poet; he was an orator, a reformer, a statesman. He was a man of faith, a man who was unsure neither of God nor of himself. He has been called "The king of all the prophets," "The evangelist of the Old Covenant," "The eagle among the prophets," "The Saint Paul of the Old Testament," "The evangelical prophet." So great a man was Isaiah that it is difficult to exaggerate when describing him.

Isaiah was born about 765 B.C. In 1:1 we are told that his father's name was Amoz (to be carefully distinguished from the prophet Amos), who, according to Jewish tradition, was a brother of Amaziah, the father of King Uzziah of Judah. If the tradition is correct, Isaiah was a nephew of King Amaziah and a

cousin of King Uzziah. In any event, his entire con-
duct and bearing lead us to believe that he was of
royal blood. He had ready access to King Ahaz (7:3)
and King Hezekiah (38:1) as well as to members of
the royal court (22:15-25) and of the priesthood (8:2).
He kept in touch with political events and was familiar with the names of palace officials (36:3). The city
of Jerusalem appears to have been his home, since he
was well acquainted with its various sections and
environs (7:3; 22:16) as well as with the character of
its people (3:1-22).

A man of no mean education (8:1; 30:8), Isaiah
wrote in an eloquent and cultured style. He composed
a history of Uzziah's reign (2 Chron. 26:22) as well as
an account of "Hezekiah's reign and his acts of devo-
tion" (32:32). In addition to writing the book of
Isaiah, he found time to train a number of disciples
(Isa. 8:16). The length of his prophetic service for the
Lord, rivaled only by that of Daniel, was at least sixty
years—from the death of Judah's King Uzziah (6:1)
in 740 B.C. to the accession of the Assyrian ruler
Esarhaddon (37:38) in 681 B.C. According to both
Jewish and Christian tradition, Isaiah met his death
by being sawed in two in a hollow log by Judah's
wicked King Manasseh (see Heb. 11:37).

His Family

Isaiah was married at least once and had at least
two children. His wife, though unnamed in the text,
was a prophetess (Isa. 8:3). His firstborn son was
named Shear-Jashub (7:3), which means "A remnant
will return." Another son bore the name Maher-Shalal-Hash-Baz (8:1,3), meaning "Quick to the plunder,
swift to the spoil." Isaiah's own name means "The
LORD saves," and his name and the names of his sons
became "signs and symbols in Israel from the LORD

Almighty" (8:18) as the history of God's people
unfolded (for Shear-Jashub, see 10:21-22; for Maher-
Shalal-Hash-Baz, see 8:4; for Isaiah himself, see
45:17).

His Times

Because of far-reaching changes both in the Holy
Land and in the surrounding lands during Isaiah's
lifetime, there were immense contrasts between the
Judah of Isaiah's earlier years and the Judah of his
later years. Wealth was transformed into poverty,
social conditions deteriorated, and the religious picture became confused. Samaria, the capital of the
northern kingdom of Israel, was destroyed by the
Assyrians in 722 B.C. and the importation of foreign
elements into the north added to the overall chaos.

On the international scene, after a long period of
relative weakness Assyria found a strong ruler in
Tiglath-Pileser III (who reigned from 745 to 727 B.C.),
the great rebuilder of the Assyrian empire. After win-
ning the support of the people of Babylonia he
marched westward, eventually to put both Israel's
King Menahem (2 Kings 15:19, where Tiglath-Pileser
is called by his Babylonian name Pul) and Judah's
King Ahaz (16:7-8) under tribute. Tiglath-Pileser's
son and successor, Shalmaneser V (727-722),
besieged the Phoenician city of Tyre for five years and
Samaria for three years (17:4-5). Although he should
be given the lion's share of the credit (or blame) for
destroying the northern kingdom of Israel, he probably died during the siege. His successor, Sargon II
(722–705), claims in his own annals that he himself
was the conqueror of Samaria. Sargon was apparently one of Shalmaneser's army commanders, and
he usurped the throne of Assyria after Shalmaneser's
death. Sargon (an assumed name) means "The king

is legitimate"—a name that becomes necessary only if its bearer is not in fact legitimate! Sargon's son and successor was Sennacherib (705–681), who invaded Judah on at least one occasion (701 B.C.). He captured "all the fortified cities of Judah" (18:13) and, according to his own chronicles, made "Hezekiah, the Jew, . . . a prisoner in Jerusalem, his royal residence, like a bird in a cage." But Sennacherib was unable to seize Jerusalem itself, because the angel of the Lord put to death 185 thousand Assyrian soldiers who had surrounded the city. The Assyrian ruler was forced to return to his capital city of Nineveh and was eventually succeeded on the throne by his son Esarhaddon (Isa. 37:36-38).

On the domestic scene, Isaiah's early years overlapped a period of unparalleled prosperity in both Israel in the north under Jeroboam II (793–753) and Judah in the south under Uzziah (792–740). (Since Isaiah was a southern prophet whose ministry was primarily to Judah and Jerusalem, we will focus our attention here on the major events that took place during the reigns of the Judahite rulers Uzziah, Jotham, Ahaz and Hezekiah [1:1].) King Uzziah (also known as Azariah) did what was right in the Lord's eyes, but he failed to remove the pagan shrines that dotted the countryside of his realm (2 Kings 15:1-4). Politically speaking, he was a powerful ruler: He rebuilt Elath on the Red Sea, fought successful battles against the Philistines, developed a well-trained army, and built towers to strengthen the walls of Jerusalem (2 Chron. 26:1-15). But late in life he entered the Temple in order to burn incense on the altar of incense, and his prideful act led to his downfall: He became a leper, was excluded from the Temple, and was forced to put the palace in charge of his son Jotham for the last ten years of his life (26:16-

21). Uzziah died in 740 B.C., the year of Isaiah's call to be a prophet (Isa. 6:1).

Like his father Uzziah, Jotham (750–732) did what was right in the Lord's eyes but failed to remove his countrymen's pagan shrines (2 Kings 15:32-38; 2 Chron. 26:23–27:9). Although Jotham "grew powerful because he walked steadfastly before the LORD his God" (2 Chron. 27:6), his son and successor, Ahaz (735–715), was a wicked ruler: He burned his sons alive as offerings to pagan deities, offered sacrifices to foreign gods, went to Tiglath-Pileser for help against the Arameans and Israelites and paid tribute to him in spite of Isaiah's warnings, brought an Aramean altar into the Jerusalem Temple, and eventually shut the doors of the Temple and set up altars at every street corner in Jerusalem (2 Kings 15:38–16:20; 2 Chron. 27:9–28:26). So sinful a king was Ahaz that when he was buried "he was not placed in the tombs of the kings of Israel" (2 Chron. 28:27).

Ahaz's son Hezekiah (715–686), by contrast, was a godly king (2 Kings 18–20; 2 Chron. 28:27–32:33), and four chapters of Isaiah's prophecy are devoted to events in Hezekiah's reign (Isa. 36–39). In the first month of his rule Hezekiah opened the doors of the Lord's Temple and had the building purified and consecrated. He and his great-grandson Josiah were the only two kings in Judah's history worthy of the title "reformer." Because of Hezekiah's rebellion against Assyria, Sennacherib invaded Judah in 701 B.C. but was unable to capture Jerusalem. In his later years Hezekiah fell sick, and Isaiah came to tell him that he would die. Hezekiah pleaded for his life, however, and the Lord granted him fifteen additional years (2 Kings 20:1-11; Isa. 38:1-8).

Manasseh (697–642), Hezekiah's son and successor, was even more wicked than his grandfather Ahaz had been. During his long and cruel reign the streets of Jerusalem ran red with the blood of the prophets (2 Kings 21:1-18; 2 Chron. 33:1-10), and Jewish and Christian tradition assures us that Isaiah himself was martyred under him (as mentioned earlier). The eventual humbling and repentance of Manasseh were too little and too late (2 Chron. 33:11-20).

His Task

Although Isaiah's ministry was to be one of fruitless warning concerning judgment to come (Isa. 6:9-13), he dedicated himself (6:8), his family (8:18) and his disciples (8:16) to it. His message was primarily to Judah and Jerusalem, but he spoke also to the northern kingdom of Israel (9:8–10:4; 17:1-11; 28:1-6) as well as to foreign nations (13–23). In addition to being a preacher par excellence, Isaiah also taught through the use of parables (5:1-7; 28:23-29). During one period of his life he went around stripped and barefoot for three years to symbolize the humiliation of captives from Egypt and the upper Nile region (20:2-6).

THE BOOK

Its Author

Until about the twelfth century A.D. no one seriously questioned the fact that the prophet Isaiah wrote the entire book that bears his name. Since the days of the Jewish commentator Ibn Ezra (A.D. 1092–1167), however, many Old Testament scholars have concluded that Isaiah 40–66 (and perhaps also other sections, such as 24–27) could not have been written by the same person who composed Isaiah 1–39. It is claimed that Isaiah 1–39 differs from Isaiah 40–66 in its choice of themes, subject matter, literary style, and theological teachings. Even more important, Isaiah 40–66 pictures the kingdom of Judah as living in exile in Babylon after Jerusalem's destruction in 586 B.C.—about a century after Isaiah's death.

But differences in theme, subject matter and so forth do not necessarily demand differences in authorship. As we stated earlier, Isaiah's ministry extended over a period of sixty years, and so it is understandable that his developing insights concerning God's purposes for Judah and the nations of the world would undergo significant changes (and change does not always imply contradiction). Also, what is to prevent a divinely inspired author from looking a hundred years into the future and comforting his countrymen in exile—or, for that matter, predicting events that would take place centuries or even millennia later?

Apart from such observations, however, several striking features tie the two halves of Isaiah together and make it virtually certain that Isaiah 1–39 and 40–66 were written by the same author. Isaiah's name is the only one attached to the book (see 1:1; 2:1; 13:1), which means that if he did not write 40–66 we have no idea who the author of those sublime chapters was. But early evidence that he in fact wrote them is extensive, including the pre-Christian apocryphal book Ecclesiasticus (48:22-25), the first-century Jewish historian Josephus (*Antiquities* XI,i,2), and several of the Church fathers. Verbal parallels between 1–39 and 40–66 are numerous (compare 1:2 with 66:24; 5:27 with 40:30; 6:1 with 52:13 and 57:15; 6:11-12 with 62:4; 11:1 with 53:2; 11:6-9 with 65:25; 11:12 with 49:22; 35:10 with 51:11). The literary structure of the book as a whole (see below) argues for its unity.

In addition, many passages in the New Testament refer to the prophet Isaiah in connection with various parts of 40–66: Matthew 3:3 and Luke 3:4 quote from Isaiah 40:3; Matthew 12:17-21 quotes from Isaiah 42:1-4; Romans 10:16 and 20 quote from Isaiah 53:1 and 65:1; and, most impressive of all, John 12:38-41 quotes from Isaiah 53:1 and then from 6:10, thus tying the two halves of the book together under Isaiah's name.

Another strong argument for the unity of the book of Isaiah is the phrase "Holy One of Israel," a name for God that appears twenty-six times in Isaiah but only five times elsewhere in the Old Testament (Ps. 71:22; 78:41; 89:18; Jer. 50:29; 51:5). The occurrences in Isaiah are divided almost equally between the two halves—twelve times in 1–39 (1:4; 5:19; 5:24; 10:20; 12:6; 17:7; 29:19; 30:11; 30:12; 30:15; 31:1; 37:23 [= 2 Kings 19:22, which therefore does not really count as another occurrence outside Isaiah]) and fourteen times in 40–66 (41:14; 41:16; 41:20; 43:3; 43:14; 45:11; 47:4; 48:17; 49:7 [twice]; 54:5; 55:5; 60:9; 60:14). We see, then, that "Holy One of Israel" is virtually Isaiah's special name for God, whether in 1–39 or in 40–66.

One final point: The oldest known manuscript of Isaiah, discovered in 1947 in a cave near the Dead Sea, dates to about 150 B.C. It displays a section break between chapters 33 and 34 (a logical place for such a division) but none between 39 and 40. The main Dead Sea scroll of Isaiah thus gives no indication that the book might have been written by more than one author.

In summary, there are compelling reasons for continuing to hold the traditional view that all sixty-six chapters of Isaiah were written by the prophet himself.

Its Date

Most of the events in chapters 1–39 were probably recorded by Isaiah during his earlier years of ministry (see 6:1; 14:28; 36:1), although a few of them may have been written down in his later years. As we hinted above, Isaiah doubtless wrote chapters 40–66 during the last few years of his life. The time span between these two periods of writing adequately accounts for the differences between 1–39 and 40–66.

Its Literary Structure

The prophecy of Isaiah may be divided into seven basic literary units of varying length: (1) the Book of Immanuel, 1–12; (2) the Book of Oracles Against the Nations, 13–23; (3) the Book of Apocalyptic Oracles, 24–27; (4) the Book of Woes, 28–33; (5) the Book of Judgment and Restoration, 34–35; (6) the Book of Hezekiah, 36–39; and (7) the Book of Consolation, 40–66. The Book of Hezekiah is an historical interlude serving as a key transitional section that both concludes 1–35 and introduces 40–66. Here now is a more detailed outline of the entire book of Isaiah:

  I. The Book of Immanuel (1–12)
     A.   The Great Arraignment (1)
     B.   Jerusalem Present and Future (2–4)
     C.   The Song of the Vineyard (5)
     D.   The Prophet's Call (6)
     E.   Judah and Immanuel (7:1–9:7)
     F.   Ephraim and the Lord (9:8–10:4)
     G.   Assyria and Messiah (10:5–12:6)
  II. The Book of Oracles Against the Nations (13–23)
     A.   Babylon (13:1–14:27; 21:1-10)
     B.   Philistia (14:28-32)

We will deviate only slightly from this outline in the commentary that follows.

Its Theme and Purpose

The prophet Isaiah was a contemporary of three other prophets: Hosea, Amos and Micah. A comparison of the opening verses of each of their prophetic books helps us to reconstruct their chronological order: Amos, Hosea, Isaiah, Micah. The youngest of the four prophets—Micah—summarizes the basic messages of his three older contemporaries in a memorable verse (Mic. 6:8): "What does the LORD require of you? To act justly [see Amos 5:24] and to love mercy [see Hosea 6:6] and to walk humbly with your God [see Isa. 29:19]." A fundamental purpose of the book of Isaiah is to stress the fact that God's people should be humble in His exalted presence (see also Isa. 2:11,17; 5:15-16).

In our commentary we will be looking at many themes that Isaiah is concerned about in this remarkable prophecy. But does he have a major theme that holds all the other themes together?

We cannot go far wrong if we remind ourselves again that Isaiah's name means "the LORD saves" and conclude that the primary theme of the book of Isaiah is salvation. Isaiah 45:22, then, can serve us well as a theme verse for the book as a whole: "Turn to me and be saved, all you ends of the earth; for I am God, and there is no other."

2

ISAIAH'S CALL

Isaiah 6

The Lord is "a God who hides himself" (Isa. 45:15). No matter how hard we try, all of our efforts to understand God are doomed to failure. His plans and purposes are a mystery to us, because His thoughts and ways are higher than ours (55:8-9). If we are ever to know God, it will only be because He has decided to reveal Himself to us (Deut. 29:29). When we search for God in our own strength—that is, when the direction of the search is from down upward—we cannot succeed. It is only when God seeks us—that is, when the direction of the search is from up downward—that contact between God and ourselves can be made.

The call of God to His people, then, is basic to biblical faith. Every man-made religion is founded on the principle that it is possible for people to reach out and touch God through their own initiative. But revealed religion, as taught in the Bible, affirms that our relationship to God is based on divine grace and not on human activity. Revelation takes place only when God discloses Himself to us.

The Hebrew word translated "prophet" is *navi* (pronounced nah-VEE), a term that means literally "one who has been called." Abraham was the first person in the Old Testament to bear the title of prophet (Gen. 20:7), and God called him to leave his father's household and serve Him (12:1-3). Moses was among the greatest of all the prophets (Deut. 18:15-18), and from within a burning bush God called him (Exod. 3:4). The Bible contains numerous accounts of other prophetic calls as well, such as those of Jeremiah (1:4-19), Ezekiel (2:1–3:15), Hosea (1:2–3:5) and Amos (7:14-15). We observe that in each case the man became a prophet not by human preference but through divine choice. True prophecy is a vocation (which means "calling"), not a profession (which depends on human initiative).

Since Isaiah was a prophet (Isa. 37:2; 38:1; 39:3-4) we might have expected him to give us the story of his call, and he has not disappointed us. In fact, the sixth chapter of his prophecy is an outstanding example of a "call" narrative because it describes the basic elements of what a person can expect to happen when he or she is called by God to serve Him. A called person can anticipate seeing the Lord as He really is (6:1-4), then seeing oneself as he or she really is (6:5-8), and finally, seeing the world as it really is (6:9-13). Because Isaiah's call doubtless took place at the very outset of his prophetic ministry, we will comment on Isaiah 6 here and then turn to Isaiah 1–5 in our next chapter.

SEEING THE LORD (Isa. 6:1-4)

The year was 740 B.C., and Judah's King Uzziah was dead after a reign of 52 years in Jerusalem (2 Chron. 26:3). His name means "The LORD is my strength," and his other name, Azariah (2 Kings 15:1-2), means "The LORD has helped." Both names were appropriate to his career, because we read of him that "he was greatly helped until he became powerful" (2 Chron. 26:15). Unfortunately, however, his strength became his weakness when "his pride led to his downfall" (26:16). In his later life he was unfaithful to the Lord and was forced to spend his final years in shame and disgrace (26:16-23).

Isaiah's call to prophesy came to him in the year that Uzziah died. Uzziah's reign had been long and prosperous, and Isaiah and his fellow Israelites must have wondered what would happen now that the throne was empty. And so, as if to quiet their fears, a divine vision of a throne was granted to the prophet, and seated on the throne was the Lord Himself in His heavenly temple (see Ps. 11:4). In contrast to the lowly Uzziah, the Lord is "high and exalted" (Isa. 6:1; see 57:15). And in contrast to the human Uzziah, the Lord whom Isaiah saw was none other than Jesus Himself in a pre-incarnation appearance, because John 12:39-41, after quoting Isaiah 6:10, says that "Isaiah said this because he saw Jesus' glory and spoke about him."

Above the heavenly throne and its divine occupant were "seraphs" (Isa. 6:2), who appear only here in Scripture. The word *seraph* probably means "burning one," either in reference to their purity as servants in God's throne room or to stress their relationship to the altar from which one of them was about to take a "live coal" (6:6). Like the "four living creatures" in Revelation 4:8, each of the seraphs had six wings. With two wings they "covered their faces" (in reverence), with two they "covered their feet" (perhaps bowing down in humility), and with two they were flying (in service). Reverence pertains to seeing the Lord (see 6:1-4), humility relates to seeing oneself (see 6:5-8), and service involves seeing the world (see 6:9-13), so the activity of the seraphs matches the outline of Isaiah 6 as determined earlier.

The seraphs were calling back and forth to each other: "Holy, holy, holy is the LORD Almighty; the whole earth is full of his glory" (6:3). The threefold "holy" was used for emphasis (see Jer. 7:4; 22:29) and perhaps also to prefigure the New Testament doctrine of the Trinity (see Rev. 4:8). The second line of the seraphs' song—"The whole earth is full of his glory"—reminds us of the words of another angelic choir centuries later: "Glory to God in the highest" (Luke 2:13). It is always true, as the Westminster Confession puts it, that "the chief end of man [and seraphs!] is to glorify God and to enjoy him forever." The phrase in the song of the seraphs is reminiscent of Numbers 14:21 ("The glory of the LORD fills the whole earth") and Psalm 72:19 ("May the whole earth be filled with his glory"). To this thought Isaiah himself adds the observation that some day "the earth will be full of the *knowledge* of the LORD" (Isa. 11:9), and Habakkuk 2:14 later combines the two ideas: "The earth will be filled with the *knowledge* of the *glory* of the LORD." Although that day has not yet come, we as Christians long for it, for the day when we can sing, "You are worthy, our Lord and God, to receive glory and honor and power, for you created all things, and by your will they were created and have their being" (Rev. 4:11).

The sound of the seraphic voices made the doorposts and thresholds shake (Isa. 6:4), but the remarkable parallel in Revelation 15:8 leads us to believe that "the temple was filled with smoke" because of God's glory and power. Smoke often accompanied visible appearances of the Lord (see Gen. 15:17; Exod. 19:18).

After seeing the Lord—high and exalted, attended by seraphs, holy and glorious and powerful—Isaiah would never be the same again.

SEEING HIMSELF (Isa. 6:5-8)

Isaiah pronounced six woes on his countrymen
(Isa. 5:8, 11, 18, 20, 21, 22), but once he had seen
the Lord as He really is Isaiah was compelled to pronounce a seventh woe—on himself: "Woe to me!"
(6:5). He had learned that no one can catch a glimpse
of God's glory without recognizing his own lostness
and ruin (see Luke 5:8). And he now understood also
that sin manifests itself most clearly in what we say
and express verbally in other ways, that the disease of
sin concentrates its poisonous influence in the lips:
"I am a man of unclean lips" (Isa. 6:5). Maybe Isaiah
was comparing himself to Moses, who knew himself
to be a man who spoke with "uncircumcised lips"
(Exod. 6:12, 30). Our sinful natures are more appar-
ent in what we say with our lips, our tongues, our
mouths (Isa. 59:3; Jer. 9:8, Matt. 12:34; Jas. 3:8)
than in anything else we do.

Isaiah knew that sin is a social matter as well as
an individual matter, and he knew also that if he was
to represent his people before God he must confess
their sins as well as his own: "I am a man of unclean
lips, and I live among a people of unclean lips" (Isa.
6:5). And what had brought Isaiah to the realization
that he and his people were sinners through and
through? He tells us: "My eyes have seen the King,
the Lord Almighty." The king of Israel was dead, but
the King of heaven was very much alive. Because
Isaiah had seen God as He really is, he was able to see
himself and his people—by contrast—as they really
were.

But the remedy for Isaiah's sense of unworthiness
was near at hand. A seraph, a messenger of the
divine love, flew to him from the Temple altar with a

live coal in his hand, and with it he touched Isaiah's lips—the very lips that Isaiah had confessed were unclean. The seraph then said to him, "Your guilt is taken away and your sin atoned for" (6:7). The healing and cauterizing flame did its purifying work, because fire not only sears—it also sublimates. Before his experience of forgiveness Isaiah could have said with the psalmist, "Heal me, for I have sinned against you" (Ps. 41:4). Isaiah had confessed his sin and had been answered by the One who "is faithful and just and will forgive us our sins and purify us from all unrighteousness" (1 John 1:9).

When the seraph touched Isaiah's mouth, the ultimate purpose was to enable Isaiah to prophesy, as in the case of two later prophets (see Jer. 1:9, Dan. 10:16). The removal of sin is always followed by the requirement of service. Commission always follows cleansing. We have been saved to serve.

The cornerstone of the classroom building at Bethel Theological Seminary in Saint Paul, Minnesota, quotes the Lord's question and Isaiah's answer as recorded in Isaiah 6:8: "Whom shall I send? . . . Here am I! Send me!" God's servants are asked to respond to Him today just as Isaiah did centuries ago—in forgiveness, in freedom, in faith. Like Paul, Isaiah "was not disobedient to the vision from heaven" (Acts 26:19).

But although in one sense Isaiah responded freely to God's call, in another sense he was commanded, he was compelled, he was under marching orders—he could do nothing other than speak out for his Lord. He could have echoed the words of Amos 3:8 ("The Sovereign LORD has spoken—who can but prophesy?") as, in effect, Paul did in 1 Corinthians 9:16: "I am compelled to preach. Woe to me if I do not preach the gospel!" We must always insist that sin forgiven leads to service joyful, and the lives of all who are called by the Lord must reflect the words of the psalmist: "Save me from bloodguilt, O God, the God who saves me, and my tongue will sing of your righteousness. O Lord, open my lips, and my mouth will declare your praise" (Ps. 51:14-15).

SEEING THE WORLD (Isa. 6:9-13)

Isaiah experienced conviction: "I am a man of unclean lips" (6:5).

Isaiah experienced cleansing: "Your guilt is taken away" (6:7).

Isaiah experienced consecration: "Here am I. Send me!" (6:8).

And now, Isaiah experienced commissioning: "Go and tell" (6:9).

The Lord told Isaiah that the prophet's audience would be not "my people" (they refused to obey God and enjoy a personal relationship with Him) but "this people" (6:9-10). It is a sobering thought indeed that Isaiah 6:9-10 is quoted in whole or in part in each of the first six books of the New Testament. Jesus (Matt. 13:14-15; Mark 4:12; Luke 8:10) knew that His parables, while helping some to understand His message and mission, would serve only to drive others far from Him. John had the same insight with respect to Jesus' message (John 12:39-40), and Paul misunderstood it to be true of his own preaching as well (Acts 28:25-27; Romans 11:8). What was true in Isaiah's day is true in every age: Some listen, some refuse to listen—but still we must spread the good news (see Ezek. 3:11). As the commission was to Isaiah, so it will always be to the man or woman of God's choosing: "Go, regardless of the consequences!"

That Isaiah 6:10 is a literary gem would be denied only by the least sensitive of us, because its structure

is a beautiful example of what is called inversion:
"heart . . . ears . . . eyes; . . . eyes . . . ears . . . heart."
But its primary purpose lies in its content, not its
form. It emphasizes the truth that "there are none so
blind as those who will not see." It declares that in
every age there are Pharisees to whom God's Son
must say, "For judgment I have come into this world,
so that the blind will see and those who see will
become blind" (John 9:39). A message like this is
never easy to proclaim, however, and Isaiah was concerned to know the length of his term of prophecy:
"For how long, O Lord?" (Isa. 6:11). God's response
was pessimistic in the extreme, describing terrible
retribution: Cities, houses, fields, people—indeed,
the entire land—would be ruined and ravaged and
utterly forsaken (6:11-12).

Was there then no hope at all? There would seem
to be at least a glimmer: a tenth, a holy seed, a stump
(6:13). Two sturdy Near Eastern trees, the terebinth
and the oak, can sprout from the stump even after
being felled. Isaiah's teaching concerning the remnant shines forth at this point. Even in the worst of
circumstances the Lord "left us some survivors" (1:9).
Although merely a stump, "a remnant of the house of
Judah will take root below and bear fruit above. For
out of Jerusalem will come a remnant, and out of
Mount Zion a band of survivors" (37:31-32). How
would such an event be possible? The answer is given
immediately: "The zeal of the Lord Almighty will
accomplish this" (37:32). And it is to such a remnant
that we have the opportunity and challenge of minis-
tering today. Paul reminds us that "at the present
time there is a remnant chosen by grace" (Rom.
11:5). To the root, to the shoot, to the natural
branches, to the ingrafted branches (11:16-24) we
must present the gospel. And we can do so only by

hastening, in response to God's call, to cover our faces in reverence before him, to cover our feet in humility and confession, and to "soar on wings like eagles" in service, so that we may "run and not grow weary," that we may "walk and not be faint" (Isa. 40:31). When we have seen God as He really is, and when we have seen ourselves as we really are, only then can we truly see the world and its needs—as Isaiah did.

Hope

THEMES FROM ISAIAH 6

What spiritual truths were impressed on Isaiah as a result of his call?

God is holy. In Hebrew thought "to be holy" meant "to be separated," "to be set apart," "to be at a distance." When an ancient Israelite referred to God as "holy" (Isa. 6:3), he meant that no other being in heaven or on earth can compare with Him: " 'To whom will you compare me? Or who is my equal?' says the Holy One" (40:25). God is unapproachable: "Who can stand in the presence of the LORD, this holy God?" (1 Sam. 6:20). He is different from and contrasted with mankind: "I am God, and not man—the Holy One among you" (Hos. 11:9). At the same time, however, His holiness does not prevent Him from being good and gracious and kind and loving to all who are "contrite and lowly in spirit" (Isa. 57:15). Through His promises we are able to "participate in the divine nature" (2 Pet. 1:4). Because of God's holiness, in the Old Testament period there were holy days, a holy city, a holy temple, a holy priesthood, a holy people.

God is powerful. He is the "LORD Almighty" (Isa. 6:5), a phrase that means literally "LORD of Hosts." The name emphasizes the universality and omnipotence of the God of Israel. He is the Lord of Hosts in the sense that He is the "God of the armies of Israel" (1 Sam. 17:45), the God of the "sun, the moon and the stars—all the heavenly array" (Deut. 4:19), the God whom the prophet Micaiah saw "sitting on his throne with all the host of heaven standing around him" (1 Kings 22:19), the God of the angelic choir on that first Christmas (Luke 2:13). Because He is the Lord of Hosts with respect to everything that exists (Gen. 2:1), Isaiah rightfully recognized Him as "the LORD Almighty" (compare Isa. 6:3 with Rev. 4:8). God's power and sovereignty extend over everything in heaven and on earth.

God's relationship to His people has a moral and ethical basis. Isaiah knew that his own lips and the lips of his fellow Israelites were "unclean" (Isa. 6:5), impure, polluted, and that only God could rectify the situation and cleanse them. Before Isaiah's experience of forgiveness he was a man of "guilt" (6:7), a word that means "crookedness, distortion, perversion." His countrymen, also, were "loaded with guilt" (1:4). Isaiah was unable to serve the Lord until his "sin" was atoned for (6:7). In the Old Testament, "sin" is the most common term for man's disobedient attitudes toward and actions against God. It means "missing the mark" (the same root is used of Benjamite marksmen in Judg. 20:16), "falling short" of a goal or target (Paul expresses the same idea in Rom. 3:23). The presence of sin in the life of a believer makes fellowship with and service for God impossible.

Only God can initiate atonement and forgiveness. The seraph was the Lord's messenger to effect reconciliation between Isaiah and his God (Isa. 6:6-7). The "live coal" reminds us that fire in the Bible often symbolizes the destruction of what is evil (33:14) and the purification of what is good. God is the only One who is able "to forgive," a verb that means "to remove," "to take away." He is the only One who can provide "atonement," a noun that means "covering," "cancellation," "blotting out." The Lord taught Isaiah that in order to be a prophet, one must know atonement and forgiveness as an experience and not only as a doctrine.

A prophet's audience is often stubborn and corrupt. Isaiah 6:9-10 does not portray the purpose of Isaiah's message but its results. Even in the days of Jesus Christ, the light of the world, "men loved darkness instead of light because their deeds were evil" (John 3:19). But as in Isaiah's case, so also in ours, we are commanded only to proclaim God's truth, not to guarantee its results.

God's judgment against unconfessed sin is inevitable. In the days of Noah, God said that He would "send rain on the earth for forty days and forty nights" (Gen. 7:4), and He kept His promise (7:12). He said that He would "wipe from the face of the earth every living creature" He had made (7:4), and He did so (7:23). Isaiah 6:11-12 describes the terrible destruction that would overtake the people of Judah because of their sin. And, of course, judgment against sin is not limited to our life on earth: "Man is destined to die once, and after that to face judgment" (Heb. 9:27).

God preserves a faithful remnant. In Scripture generally and in Isaiah specifically, judgment is neither God's last nor best word. Just as the Lord saved Noah and seven others from the judgment of the flood, so also He gives His obedient children the grace to overcome whatever trials they meet in this life and the assurance of salvation on that final day of judgment. The doctrine of the faithful remnant is one of Isaiah's most important and characteristic emphases

(Isa. 6:13; see 1:9; 10:19-22; 11:1; 27:6; 37:31-32). He named his firstborn son Shear-Jashub (7:3), which means "A remnant will return." Despite the fact that Uzziah, the ruler of Judah, had died, and despite the fact that dangerous days lay just ahead, Isaiah would soon learn that he who sits on heaven's throne would rule over His people in justice and righteousness.

The king is dead.

Long live the King!

For Study or Discussion

► 1. Give some other examples from Scripture where a visionary confrontation with God resulted in a sudden awareness of sin on the part of the witness. Where else was forgiveness immediately followed by a call to service?

2. What are we responsible to do in order to see God as He really is? Ourselves as we really are? Support your answer with Scripture.

3. Compare Matthew 13:10-17 with Isaiah 6:9-10. How do these passages of Scripture illuminate one another?

4. How did the stubbornness of Isaiah's audience differ from that of the Pharisees?

5. List other Bible verses that illustrate the purifying nature of fire or its destructive effect over evil.

3

ISAIAH'S MISSION

Isaiah 1—5

The story of Isaiah's call to be a prophet of the Lord (Isa. 6) divides the Book of Immanuel (1—12) into two parts: 1—5 and 7—12. When Isaiah was given his divine commission, God told him that most of his hearers would be sinful people who would pay no attention to his message and would eventually be judged for their wickedness. Sin and judgment—these are the twin themes that weave their way throughout the account of Isaiah's mission in Isaiah 1—5, the first half of the Book of Immanuel.

THE GREAT ARRAIGNMENT (Isa. 1)

Chronologically, Isaiah 1—5 probably describes the situation in Judah and Jerusalem shortly after Isaiah's call, which took place in "the year that King Uzziah died" (6:1). The reign of Jotham, then, is the background of these chapters.

Although Jotham himself seems to have been a good ruler as well as a devout believer in the Lord (2 Chron. 27:6), he failed to destroy the pagan shrines that worshipers of foreign gods had built in Judah. His people therefore "continued to offer sacrifices and burn incense there" (2 Kings 15:35). In short, they "continued their corrupt practices" (2 Chron. 27:2).

"Corrupt"—Isaiah could not think of a more adequate word to describe his sinful countrymen: They were wicked people indeed, "children given to corruption" (Isa. 1:4). Such flagrant sin could not go unpunished, and the Lord called on heaven and earth to witness (1:2) as He arraigned His people before the bar of justice and entered into judgment against them (3:13-14).

What had they done? What was God accusing them of? Disobedience (1:2); refusing to acknowledge their Creator (1:3); rejecting the Holy One of Israel (1:4); bringing the Lord "meaningless offerings" (1:13); turning their sacred meetings into "evil assemblies" (1:13); committing murder (1:15,22); engaging in theft and bribery (1:23); ignoring the pleas of women and children who lacked adequate support and legal representation (1:23); worshiping at pagan shrines (1:29)—the list goes on and on.

Because of their sin the people were already experiencing God's hand of judgment. They were suffering like a sick man, covered with "wounds and welts and open sores" (1:6). The fields and villages of Judah were being laid waste by foreigners (1:7). Jerusalem herself, the "Daughter of Zion" (the temple mount), had become like the flimsiest shack (1:8). Only God's mercy had kept her from being overthrown like Sodom and Gomorrah (1:9; see Gen. 19:24-25)—even though Jerusalem justly deserved to bear the infamous name of Sodom (Isa. 1:10; 3:9; see also Rev. 11:8) because of her wickedness (Isa. 1:21-24). At one time she had been "the faithful city," but now she was no better than a prostitute (1:21).

Isaiah made full use of his literary talents in pointing out the only two options available to the people of

Judah. He was fond of employing Hebrew words that could have one meaning in one context and the opposite in another. If the people obeyed the Lord, Isaiah told them, they would "eat" the best from the land (1:19); but if they disobeyed, they would be "devoured" by the sword (1:20). Their sin would cause God to "turn" His hand against them (1:25); His grace would "restore" their leaders as in days of old (1:26).

One of our former presidents, Lyndon B. Johnson, had the opening words of Isaiah 1:18 displayed prominently in the Oval Office: "Come now, let us reason together." His intent was to portray himself as a reasonable man, the better to arrive at compromise in the halls of Congress. Needless to say, the Lord's original purpose in calling His people to the bar of reason was much more radical and thoroughgoing: Their sins were red because their hands were "full of blood" (1:15), but if they sincerely repented God would transform their lives and make them as pure and white as the driven snow (1:18; see also Ps. 51:7). Then their beloved and beautiful Jerusalem would once again deserve to be called "the City of Righteousness, the Faithful City" (1:26).

Isaiah's mission was to warn the people that God, the "Judge of all the earth" (Gen. 18:25), would sentence them to destruction unless they turned from sin and to Him.

JERUSALEM PRESENT AND FUTURE (Isa. 2—4)

Eschatological Jerusalem (2:1-5)

Almost word for word, Isaiah's younger contemporary, Micah, shared with the great prophet this astounding vision of a world at peace (Mic. 4:1-3). The Lord's Temple in Jerusalem will be elevated above all earthly things, and all the nations will stream to it in order to learn His ways and understand His word and will. Reversing the command of another prophet on another occasion (see Joel 3:10), Isaiah predicted that every weapon of war would become an instrument of peace (Isa. 2:4).

In the plaza outside the United Nations headquarters building in New York City, an enormous statue strikingly depicts a powerful blacksmith beating "swords into plowshares." But such a long-hoped-for event will not take place until the *eschaton*, the end of history, "the last days" (Isa. 2:2), in God's own time. Meanwhile we can say, with Saint Francis of Assisi, "Lord, make me an instrument of thy peace." By so doing we will, in the words of Isaiah, be walking "in the light of the LORD" (2:5).

Contemporary Jerusalem (2:6—4:1)

Once again Isaiah returned to his emphasis on the truth that human sin inevitably results in divine judgment. The threat of God's retribution is evident in 2:6-22. The prosperity of Jotham's reign was probably scarcely less than that of his father Uzziah and gave the people time to indulge in pagan superstitions (2:6), luxury (2:7a), military ventures (2:7b), and—worst of all—idolatry. Worship of idols was the most serious sin committed by the Israelites, and each of the three times Isaiah mentioned it here (2:8,18,20) it was followed by the need of idol-worshipers to flee "from dread of the LORD and the splendor of his majesty" (2:10,19,21). One of God's names is "Jealous" (Exod. 34:14), and He tolerates no competitors for His allegiance (Matt. 6:24).

Expanding on one of his basic themes—that God's people should be humble, and that only the Lord Himself should be exalted (Isa. 2:11,17; 5:15-

16)—Isaiah announced divine judgment against all that is mighty (2:12), whether natural objects (2:13-14) or human projects (2:15-16). Man himself, who is of no account, was not to be trusted by the people of Jerusalem and Judah (2:22). In fact, God would soon take away their food and water supplies as well as the very pillars of their society, whether military, political or religious (3:1-3), and provide only immature and incompetent leaders for them (3:4-7). The upper classes would be punished for exploiting those who were weak and poor (3:8-15). Especially singled out for judgment were (1) the men who should have been leaders but had become oppressors (3:14-15) and (2) the women of Jerusalem who should have been models of humility and gentleness but had become proud and flirtatious (3:16—4:1; see also 32:9-20; Ezek. 13:17-23; Amos 4:1-3). The time would come, Isaiah warned, when so many of Judah's men would die in battle that seven women would take hold of one man and ask to be called by his name (Isa. 4:1).

Remnant Jerusalem (4:2-6)

But punishment often precedes blessing, and judgment is never God's final word to the faithful few who trust Him completely. The survivors among His people, those who were left in Jerusalem, would some day become the recipients of divine grace (4:2-3). As in the days of the Exodus, the Lord would protect them with "a cloud of smoke by day and a glow of flaming fire by night" (4:5). As in the time of the desert wanderings, He would provide them with "a shelter and shade from the heat of the day" (4:6).

And eventually, said Isaiah, the "Branch of the LORD" would come, the Messiah Himself (4:2; see also Jer. 23:5; 33:15). After the Babylonian exile of the people of Judah, David's descendant Zerubbabel would fulfill the role of the Branch in a preliminary way (Zech. 3:8; 4:9; 6:12), but ultimately Jesus Christ, David's greatest descendant (Matt. 1:1), would be the Messiah and Saviour of all the world's people (John 3:16). Zechariah's "Here is the man" (Zech. 6:12), referring to Zerubbabel, would be answered by Pontius Pilate's "Here is the man" (John 19:5), referring to the Lord Jesus.

Isaiah's mission was to pronounce divine judgment on unrepentant unbelievers and to announce future blessing to all who placed their confidence in the Lord and were determined to live holy lives.

THE SONG OF THE VINEYARD (Isa. 5)

The Parable Itself (5:1-6)

In ancient Israel, a vineyard required proportionately more time and care than any other agricultural enterprise (5:2). Its owner therefore would be justifiably disappointed—and even angry—if his vines produced bad grapes rather than good. In such a situation he might be tempted to simply abandon it or even destroy it (5:4-6).

In the case of the vineyard about which Isaiah spoke, the owner "had a vineyard on a fertile hillside" (5:1). But despite the most careful preparation on his part, it yielded "bad fruit" (5:2), the Hebrew for which means literally "shameful things." His rhetorical question (5:4) indicates that he had done everything necessary to assure a good crop, but to no avail. So the vineyard that had originally shown such promise would be destroyed, trampled down and turned into a desolate wasteland (5:5-6).

Its Interpretation (5:7)

What does the vineyard represent, and who is its

owner? The vineyard was "the house of Israel," "the men of Judah," and the owner was "the LORD Almighty." And what kind of "fruit" did the men of Judah produce? In the song itself, the owner had "looked for" one thing "but" received another (5:2), and the Lord did the same: He "looked for justice, but saw bloodshed; for righteousness, but heard cries of distress." Isaiah made use of a pair of striking puns to drive the point home. The Lord looked for "justice"—Hebrew *mishpat* (pronounced mish-PAHT), but saw "bloodshed"—Hebrew *mispakh* (pronounced miss-PAHKH); he looked for "righteousness"—*tsedaqah* (pronounced tseh-dah-KAH), but heard "cries of distress"—*tse'aqah* (pronounced tseh-ah-KAH). The fruit of Judah's behavior was, if anything, even more shameful than the bad fruit in the parable itself.

Its Application (5:8-30)

Isaiah 5:8-23 has been described as Judah's "Grapes of Wrath" because of its series of six woes hurled against six groups of people who were responsible for producing "fruit" that was shameful in the Lord's eyes.

The first woe (5:8-10) was pronounced on the insatiable greed of land speculators who were trying to gain a monopoly over Judah's real estate in order to control its use. Isaiah's contemporary, Micah, indicated that the practice was being undertaken illegally and fraudulently (Mic. 2:1-2) and that it was causing hardship to women and children (2:9).

The second woe (Isa. 5:11-17) was leveled against drunken carousers and revelers who were concerned only about their own pleasure and had no regard for the Lord. Priests and prophets alike participated in the same kind of shameful activity (28:7-8).

The third woe (5:18-19) was spoken to presumptuous people who brazenly defied the Lord because of their unbelief. A century later their descendants in Jerusalem reflected a similar complacency (Zeph. 1:12), and even after the Babylonian exile the people of Judah remained skeptical about whether it made sense to serve God (Mal. 3:13-15).

The fourth woe (5:20) came as a warning to anyone who insisted on blurring the distinction between right and wrong, darkness and light, bitter and sweet. Incredible as it may seem, the perverse rulers of Jerusalem had entered into a covenant with death and had made falsehood their hiding place (28:14-15).

The fifth woe (5:21) was declared against all who were self-confident and conceited, all who were "wise in their own eyes and clever in their own sight." Isaiah found it necessary to lash out against such sinful arrogance again and again (29:15; 30:1; 31:1-3; see also Jer. 9:23-24).

The sixth woe (Isa. 5:22-23) was similar to the second, but the sin it addressed was especially despicable because it was being practiced by judges who therefore became incapable of being fair and just in their courtroom decisions. They were also open to accepting bribes, and Judah's other leaders were equally mercenary (Mic. 3:11).

Because Judah and Jerusalem were rotten to the core, because the people as well as their leaders were sinful and corrupt, divine judgment was certain (Isa. 5:24-30). The Assyrian army would come as the Lord's agent of vengeance: The northern kingdom of Israel would be destroyed in 722 B.C., and the southern kingdom of Judah would suffer greatly as well. The awful refrain—"Yet for all this, his anger is not turned away, his hand is still upraised" (5:25; 9:12,17,21; 10:4)—ties together Isaiah's warning to

Judah (5:24-30) and his indictment of Israel
(9:8—10:4). Assyria, symbolized by "the lion," would
come, and there would be "no one to rescue" (5:29).

Isaiah's mission was to point to particular sins of
Judah as the cause of coming judgment and to spec-
ify Assyria as God's instrument of judgment.

THEMES FROM ISAIAH 1–5

Rebellion is the basic sin. Excluding the introductory title (1:1) the first verse of Isaiah's prophecy
(1:2), as well as the last verse (66:24), quotes the Lord
as saying that certain people had "rebelled against"
Him. The Hebrew verb for "rebel" was originally used
in political contexts (see for example 2 Kings 1:1) and
refers to open revolt against a superior power. The
sin of Adam and Eve in the Garden of Eden was the
sin of rebellion. Unwilling to obey God, they decided
to follow their own willful desires—and sin entered
the human race. Refusal to obey God leads either to
obeying someone else or to obeying oneself. Neither
course of action is praiseworthy, and both imply
rebellion against God. "Rebels and sinners" are mentioned in one breath in Isaiah 1:28, where they are
equated with "those who forsake the LORD."

*Worship includes both internal motivation and
external action.* The prophet Samuel was the first to
declare the important truth that "to obey is better
than sacrifice" (1 Sam. 15:22), and a long line of
psalmists and prophets following him played varia-
tions on the same theme (Ps. 40:6-8; 50:1-23; 51:15-
19; Jer. 6:20; 7:21-26; Hos. 6:3-6; 8:13; 9:4; Amos
5:21-24; Mic. 6:6-8), in at least one case with a touch
of sarcasm (Amos 4:4-5). But perhaps no one
stressed quite so strongly the absolute necessity of a
proper heart attitude on the part of the worshiper as
did Isaiah (in 29:13; 58:1-14, but most vigorously in

1:10-17). He reminded the people of Judah and Jerusalem that when they acted wickedly, the offerings they brought were a mockery to God (1:13). If they insisted on treating people unjustly, the Lord would not accept their prayers (1:15-17). The quantity and frequency of external acts of worship could not make amends for inward sinfulness (1:11-14). First and foremost, the Lord demanded complete obedience.

Israel is the Lord's vineyard, and Israelites are his vines. As figures of speech representing Israel and its people, the vineyard and its vines appear frequently in the poetry of the Old Testament (Gen. 49:22; Deut. 32:32; Ps. 80:8-16; Jer. 2:21; Ezek. 15; 17:1-15; Hos. 10:1). Although Isaiah 5:1-7 is undoubtedly the best-known passage, all of them—taken as a whole—provide especially appropriate images to portray the various relationships that can exist between God the Vinedresser and His people. When the Lord redeemed Israel, "a vine out of Egypt" (Ps. 80:8), at the time of the Exodus, its future was bright with promise. But the rebellious Israelites eventually produced "bad fruit" (Isa. 5:2,4); they turned against the Lord and became "a corrupt, wild vine" (Jer. 2:21); although "Israel was a spreading vine," the fruit it produced was for itself and for pagan gods rather than for the Lord (Hos. 10:1). Because of Jerusalem's sin her people became like "the wood of a vine" (Ezek. 15:2), which is not "useful for anything" (15:4). Shortly after Isaiah's call and commission, the Lord sorrowfully announced what He was going to do to His vineyard, the people of Judah. He would "take away its hedge," He would "break down its wall," He would "command the clouds not to rain on it" (Isa. 5:5-6). The end result would be judgment and destruction—and all because of His people's sin.

Drunkenness was prevalent in ancient Israel. Vines yielded grapes, and the grapes were often pressed into wine (see Isa. 5:2). Although wine was a common beverage in Old Testament days, it is instructive to note that its first mention is related to the drunkenness of an otherwise righteous man (Gen. 9:20-21). All too often the use of wine led to its abuse, as Isaiah never tired of pointing out. Two of the six woes in Isaiah 5 were pronounced against those who drink wine both day and night (5:11) and those who overindulge (5:22). Then as now, drunkenness led to dizziness and unsteadiness (19:14; 24:20), to loss of power and beauty and dignity (28:1,7-8). The ultimate tragedy would come at a future time when the Lord would judge the nations and cause them to stagger after they drank the cup of His wrath (63:6; see also 51:21-23).

Isaiah's mission was difficult indeed, and a lesser man would have shrunk from it. But his sense of God's call—and of God's presence at all times— enabled him to fulfill what the Lord wanted him to do. As he delivered his message of sin and judgment he was able to say, "The mouth of the LORD has spoken" (1:20).

For Study or Discussion

1. List several examples outside the book of Isaiah where rebellion was met with severe judgment.

2. Idolatry was one of the most serious sins that Isaiah addressed. What gods today compete most for our allegiance? What are some signs that these gods have succeeded?

3. What excuses are given today to justify oppression of the poor? How do the economic interests of today's oppressors differ from those of ancient Judah?

4. What other similarities can you see between the modern Church and the Judah of Isaiah's time?

5. Both Isaiah and Jesus predicted the destruction of Jerusalem. In what ways were their predictions similar? In what ways did they differ?

ISAIAH'S MESSAGE

Isaiah 7—12

Turning now to the second part of the Book of Immanuel, we focus our attention on several of the key features of Isaiah's God-given message to the citizens of Jerusalem and the people of Judah. As the background of Isaiah 1—5 was presumably the reign of Jotham son of Uzziah, so the background of Isaiah 7—12 was the reign of Ahaz son of Jotham (7:1). Although Jotham had been a reasonably good king, it would be difficult indeed to name a single redeeming quality in the life of his son Ahaz. In spite of the fact that he often found himself facing serious problems both at home and abroad, "in his time of trouble King Ahaz became even more unfaithful to the LORD" (2 Chron. 28:22).

Would Isaiah's message be able to penetrate the darkened heart of such a wicked man?

JUDAH AND IMMANUEL (Isa. 7:1—9:7)

The Failure of Ahaz (Chap. 7)

The year was 735 or 734 B.C. Tiglath-Pileser III

was the king of Assyria and was threatening the territorial security and integrity of the kingdoms to his west, primarily Aram and Israel. Rezin, the king of Aram, and Pekah son of Remaliah, the king of Israel, forged an anti-Assyrian mutual-defense alliance and tried to get Ahaz, the king of Judah, to join them. When he refused, they attacked Jerusalem but were unsuccessful in their attempt to capture it (7:1). The war itself is sometimes called the Syro-Ephraimite war because Aram is roughly equivalent to present-day Syria and "Ephraim" was another name for the northern kingdom of Israel (7:2) since it was Israel's most powerful tribe.

The threat of Aram and Israel frightened Ahaz and his people (7:2), and the king decided to inspect his water supply to make sure that Jerusalem would have enough for a long siege (7:3). Isaiah met Ahaz at the end of the aqueduct and advised him to keep calm because Rezin and Pekah (contemptuously referred to by Isaiah not by using his given name but simply as "the son of Remaliah"—7:4,5,9; 8:6) were merely "two smoldering stubs of firewood" (7:4)— more smoke than fire—soon to be plundered and destroyed by the king of Assyria (8:4). Aram and Israel had plotted to conquer Judah and put a foreigner, "the son of Tabeel" (otherwise unknown), on her throne (7:5-6), but the Lord promised Ahaz through Isaiah that Judah's enemies would fail (7:7). In fact, "within sixty-five years" Ephraim would be so thoroughly shattered that she would no longer be a people (7:8). And so it happened: By about 670 B.C. Esarhaddon king of Assyria had settled foreign colonists in Israel (a policy continued by his son Ashurbanipal), and their intermarriage with the few remaining Israelites marked the end of Ephraim as a separate people and gave birth to the mixed population known as the Samaritans (see 2 Kings 17:24-34; John 4:9).

Ahaz, said Isaiah, was not to trust in his own military might or in foreign alliances. Using a Hebrew verb with two different but related meanings (which in this case can be represented nicely in English), Isaiah told Ahaz that if he did not "stand firm" in his faith he would not "stand" at all (Isa. 7:9). The Lord, always gracious, offered to give Ahaz a sign to strengthen his faith (7:10-11). But Ahaz refused to accept the offer, giving the pious excuse that he did not want to "put the LORD to the test" (7:12; see Deut. 6:16).

God, however, was not to be denied. He gave Ahaz and his people a sign anyway, a sign that would become one of the most famous and remarkable prophecies in the entire Old Testament: "The virgin will be with child and will give birth to a son, and will call him Immanuel" (Isa. 7:14). The ultimate fulfillment would, of course, occur in the coming of Jesus Christ, born of the virgin Mary, as the New Testament clearly states (Matt. 1:22-23). But since signs given by the Lord through Isaiah were normally fulfilled within a few years (Isa. 20:3; 37:30), we would expect a preliminary fulfillment of the Immanuel sign fairly soon after it was revealed to Ahaz—and we are not disappointed, as the immediate context of the sign indicates: "Before the boy knows enough to reject the wrong and choose the right, the land of the two kings you dread will be laid waste. The LORD will bring on you and on your people and on the house of your father a time unlike any since Ephraim broke away from Judah—he will bring the king of Assyria" (7:16-17). Also, in Isaiah 8:8 Immanuel is addressed as one already born.

Can we identify the first Immanuel more precisely? I believe we can. Since Isaiah 7:10-17 is similar in form and content to 8:1-4, "Immanuel" and "Maher-Shalal-Hash-Baz" were probably two names for the same child, the first given by his mother and the second by his father. Alternate names are fairly common in Scripture (for example Naomi, "pleasant," was also called Mara, "bitter"; Ruth 1:20-21). Immanuel ("God is with us") is a name that points to salvation, while Maher-Shalal-Hash-Baz ("quick to the plunder, swift to the spoil") is a name that represents judgment. The interplay between salvation and judgment is one of the dominant themes in Isaiah 7—8. Isaiah 7:15-16 and 8:4 refer to the same period of time (two or three years, ending in 732 B.C. when the Assyrians destroyed the Aramean capital of Damascus and replaced Pekah king of Israel with Hoshea, who would rule for scarcely a decade before the northern kingdom of Israel would be obliterated). The word "sign," referring to Immanuel in 7:14, finds its echo in 8:18 where Isaiah calls himself and his children "signs" and symbols in Israel.

The eighth-century Immanuel, then, turns out to be one of Isaiah's sons. Some recent commentators have suggested that Isaiah's first wife, the mother of Shear-Jashub (7:3), had died. That would make his second wife a virgin at the time of the prediction in 7:14 where Isaiah said that the girl who was soon to become his second wife would give birth to a son, whom she would name Immanuel. Isaiah took his new bride to himself, and she bore the promised child, whom Isaiah named Maher-Shalal-Hash-Baz (8:3).

But although the first Immanuel was the prophet Isaiah's son, the greater Immanuel was the Son of God. The original "virgin" of Isaiah 7:14 had to marry before she could become pregnant, while the virgin

Mary "was found to be with child through the Holy Spirit" before she and her future husband Joseph "came together" (Matt. 1:18; see also Luke 1:34-35). Although the Israelites and Immanuel of Ahaz's day could say "God is with us" (Isa. 8:10) only in the sense that the Lord was on their side and would thwart the plans of their enemies, the greater Immanuel was and is in truth "God with us" (Matt. 1:23), Deity incarnate, God in human flesh (John 1:14). The Holy Spirit, co-author with Isaiah of his entire book, placed within Isaiah 7:14 the potential for a preliminary fulfillment in the time of Ahaz and a more glorious fulfillment more than 700 years later—and all of us are the richer for it.[1]

In the days of Ahaz, the kingdoms of Aram and Israel were already ripe for punishment (Isa. 7:16). But because of Ahaz's failure to trust the Lord completely, Judah would also suffer as a result of the Assyrian invasion (7:17). Isaiah used four vivid word-pictures to describe the desolation in Judah that would be caused by the Assyrian army: (1) The troops would come in huge numbers like flies and bees, and it would be impossible to escape from them (7:18-19); (2) just as the forcible shaving of a man's beard was considered an insult (2 Sam. 10:4-5), so also Tiglath-Pileser, like a hired razor (Isa. 7:20), would humiliate Ahaz by stripping away the silver and gold in his temple and palace (2 Kings 16:7-8); (3) the people of Judah would have to eat "curds and honey" (Isa. 7:21-22) because the Assyrian invasion would make it impossible for the farmers to work their fields; (4) "briers and thorns" (7:23-25) would cover the kingdom of Judah because of the destruction of the vineyards and farmlands.

Ahaz's unbelief had tragic consequences not only for himself but for his people as well.

The Failure of Judah (Chap. 8)

Like king, like people! History often teaches us that people are no better or worse than their leaders, and the situation before us is a case in point. The wickedness and unbelief of Ahaz infected his entire realm (8:6,11-12,14,19).

Uriah the priest, who served under King Ahaz (2 Kings 16:10-11), was one of the witnesses to a legal document drawn up by Isaiah, perhaps the marriage agreement between himself and his second wife (Isa. 8:1-2). Isaiah married a prophetess (8:3), a woman who doubtless shared his ministry with him. What a team they must have been as they worked together for the Lord! Their son's name, Maher-Shalal-Hash-Baz ("quick to the plunder, swift to the spoil"), meant that Damascus (Aram's capital; 7:8) and Samaria (Israel's capital; 7:9) would be plundered by the Assyrians (8:4), but it also implied that Judah would suffer as well (8:7-8). Symbolically, the people had rejected "the gently flowing waters of Shiloah" (8:6), perhaps referring by way of anticipation to the waters that flow even today from the Gihon spring (2 Chron. 32:30) to the Pool of Siloam (John 9:7; see also Neh. 3:15) through the tunnel cut into solid rock by the engineers of Hezekiah, Ahaz's successor, in 701 B.C. (2 Kings 20:20). Because of the people's rebellion the Lord would soon bring against them the king of Assyria, symbolized by the mighty floodwaters of the Euphrates River (Isa. 8:7). Those waters would devastate Judah and reach up to her very neck (8:8) in the days of the Assyrian king Sennacherib, but the faithfulness of Isaiah the prophet and Hezekiah the king would prevent Judah's capital—Jerusalem—from being destroyed (37:21-37). The first Immanuel had been born (8:8), and the Lord in His grace would make it possible for even His unfaithful people to say,

"God is with us" (8:10).

Sadly, however, the Lord had to warn "both houses of Israel" (the northern kingdom of Israel and the southern kingdom of Judah) that He would be "a stone that causes men to stumble and a rock that makes them fall" (8:14). Both Paul and Peter (Rom. 9:33; 1 Pet. 2:6-8) combine the truths of Isaiah 8:14 and 28:16, which teach us that either the Lord is the cornerstone of our lives or He is a rock over which we fall. The same choice that faced Judah faces us as well.

But Judah failed—and failed miserably. Isaiah urged the people to place their confidence in God (Isa. 8:9-15), but ultimately to no avail. So he then instructed his disciples to prepare themselves for the coming darkness (8:16-22). He told them to preserve his teaching—the "law" and the "testimony" (8:16,20)—so that they would later be able to prove that his predictions had come true. His own name and the names of his children would be "signs and symbols" (8:18) of the twin themes that constituted his message: judgment for the many who were unfaithful, restoration for the faithful few (see also Heb. 2:13, where the principles found in Isa. 8:17-18 are quoted and applied to Jesus and His ministry).

The Victory of the Coming Ruler (9:1-7)

The darkness at the end of Isaiah 8 is dispelled by the light that floods the beginning of Isaiah 9. Matthew 4:12-17 quotes Isaiah 9:1-2 and applies it to Christ. We can be sure that Matthew's first readers would have known the verses immediately following his quotation, especially Isaiah 9:6, and would have applied them to Jesus as well.

"The land of Naphtali" (9:1) in northern Israel was humbled indeed when the Assyrian king Tiglath-Pileser III attacked in about 734 B.C. (2 Kings 15:29). In the future, however, "Galilee of the Gentiles" would be honored when Jesus took up residence in Capernaum (Matt. 4:12-15). Salvation through His name would be "a great light" (Isa. 9:2), "a light for the Gentiles" (42:6; 49:6), as the gospel writers proclaimed (Matt. 4:16; Luke 1:79). Just as Midian was defeated (Isa. 9:4; see also 10:26) in the days of Gideon (Judg. 7:22-25), who broke their domination over Israel, so also the coming of Jesus would assure God's people that sin and death would no longer have mastery over them (Rom. 6:9,14). And all of this would be made possible because of God's great promise as outlined in Isaiah 9:6-7.

"A child is born"—born of a virgin (Matt. 1:23; Luke 1:34-35); "a son is given"—given by God (John 3:16)! Each of the Saviour's four names has two parts, which we want to examine in order: (1) Jesus is the "Wonderful Counselor," because He is more than a man and possesses divine wisdom (11:2; 28:29; Judg. 13:17-18); (2) Jesus is the "Mighty God," because He administers the universe with divine power (Isa. 11:2; Ps. 24:8; Heb. 1:3); (3) Jesus is the "Everlasting Father," because He cares for and protects His people with divine providence (Isa. 40:9-11; John 14:9-10); (4) Jesus is the "Prince of Peace," because He champions justice and infuses His people with divine wholeness (Isa. 11:4-9). Although the wicked Ahaz sat temporarily on David's throne, Jesus Christ, the "son of David" (Matt. 1:1) and "Son of the living God" (16:16), would some day begin a righteous rule that would last "forever" (Isa. 9:7).

EPHRAIM AND THE LORD (Isa. 9:8–10:4)
Although Isaiah's message was directed primarily

to Judah and Jerusalem (the southern kingdom and its capital), he also prophesied against Ephraim (the most powerful tribe, and therefore the representative, of the northern kingdom) and Samaria (its capital). His main oracles against Ephraim are found in Isaiah 28 and in the passage before us.

Isaiah 5:25 introduces us to a refrain—there applied primarily to Judah and Jerusalem—that recurs four times in 9:8–10:4: "Yet for all this, his anger is not turned away, his hand is still upraised" (9:12,17,21; 10:4). Foreign enemies would punish the pride and arrogance of Ephraim (9:8-12), divine retribution would fall on Ephraim's leaders and people alike because of their wickedness (9:13-17), internal strife would spread like a forest fire (9:18-21), and the best that could be expected for the nation's dishonest legislators was that they would be dragged off into exile (10:1-4). So sinful were the inhabitants of Ephraim, however, that in each case it could only be said of them that God's "anger is not turned away; his hand is still upraised."

ASSYRIA AND MESSIAH (Isa. 10:5–12:6)

Judgment Against Assyria (10:5-34)

We have now reached the closing years of the reign of Ahaz king of Judah. The destruction of Samaria by the Assyrians in 722 B.C. is presupposed in Isaiah 10:11. Assyria was now free to carry out her evil plans against Judah. But because Ahaz paid huge amounts of tribute to the Assyrian kings annually and submitted to their other demands as well, Assyria would not invade Judah until the reign of Ahaz's son Hezekiah. Isaiah predicted that invasion in this section of his prophecy.

The Assyrian rulers were proud and boastful

(10:8-11,13-14)—but little did they know that they were merely tools in the hands of a sovereign God (10:5)! The Lord would use an Assyrian king to humble the "godless nation" of Judah (10:6), and the symbolism in the name of Isaiah's second son, Maher-Shalal-Hash-Baz (8:3), which means "quick to the plunder, swift to the spoil," would reach its final fulfillment: The Assyrian troops would seize "loot" (Hebrew *shalal*) and snatch "plunder" (Hebrew *baz*: 10:6). The defenseless villages flanking the approaches to Jerusalem would tremble in anticipation of the Assyrian onslaught (10:28-31), and the enemy soldiers would "shake their fist" at the very walls of Jerusalem itself (10:32).

But instruments of divine judgment are not themselves exempt from divine judgment. Jerusalem would be judged by God, to be sure—but so would the king of Assyria (10:12). In 701 B.C. Sennacherib would invade Judah and besiege Jerusalem, but he would not capture the city because the Lord would "send a wasting disease upon his sturdy warriors" (10:16)—a disease inflicted on them by the angel of the Lord (see for example 2 Sam. 24:15-16; 1 Chron. 21:22,27) and resulting in the death of 185 thousand men (Isa. 37:36). Sennacherib would be forced to retreat to Assyria, where he would eventually be killed by his own sons (37:37-38). The Assyrians and their king, said Isaiah, would soon be judged by God for their wickedness and pride (10:5,12,15-19,24-27,33-34).

The Assyrian attack on Jerusalem would bring severe suffering to its citizens, but a remnant of the people would survive (37:3). The symbolism in the name of Isaiah's firstborn son, Shear-Jashub (7:3), which means "a remnant will return," would reach fulfillment (10:21-22). The "survivors of the house of

Jacob" would no longer be dependent on "him who struck them down" (10:20)—the king of Assyria— but would "truly rely on the LORD." In Romans 9:27-28 Paul quotes Isaiah 10:22-23, witnessing to the truth that in every generation God is gracious toward the faithful few who place their trust in Him.

The Kingdom of Messiah (Chap. 11)

At the end of Isaiah 10 the prophet says that the Lord will "lop off the boughs" of Assyria (10:33), and at the beginning of Isaiah 11 the prophet predicts the coming of the "Branch" (11:1), the Messiah. In 586 B.C. the Babylonians would destroy Judah, the king-dom of the dynasty of David, the son of Jesse (see 1 Sam. 16:10-13). But some day "from the stump of Jesse" a "shoot," the Messiah, would come (Isa. 11:1), the "Root of Jesse" would rule (11:10). The following statement is made concerning Jesus Christ in Mat-thew 2:23: "So was fulfilled what was said through the prophets: 'He will be called a Nazarene.' " The Hebrew word for "Nazarene" is *notsri* (pronounced noats-REE) and is related to the messianic *netser* (pronounced NAYT-ser), the Hebrew word for "Branch" in Isaiah 11:1. Although Isaiah 4:2 uses a different Hebrew word for "Branch," both verses look forward to the day when a King in David's line would come to rule with justice and righteousness, a King whom Christians the world over love and serve, the Lord Jesus Himself.

Isaiah foresaw that the Spirit of the Lord would rest on the Messiah (11:2)—the Spirit of "wisdom" and "understanding" (intellectual qualities, empha-sizing profound insight and sharpness of mind), the Spirit of "counsel" and "power" (practical qualities, emphasizing moral decisiveness and courageous strength), the Spirit of "knowledge" and "the fear of the LORD" (spiritual qualities, emphasizing the desire to know the will of God and the determination to perform it). The Messiah's rule would be so just and righteous (11:3-5) that nature itself would be transformed and peace would reign in the animal world as well (11:6-9; 65:25; Ezek. 34:25,28).

The prophecy in Isaiah 11:11-16 probably looked forward to the return of the Jews from Babylonian exile beginning in 538 B.C. As the Lord had led His people out of Egypt at the time of the Exodus (11:16), so He would "reach out his hand a second time" (11:11) and once again "gather the exiles" to their ancestral homeland (11:12; see also 49:22; 56:8). They would travel in triumph and with joy, back to the land of promise, along a highway free of obstacles (11:16; 57:14; 62:10).

Two Songs of Deliverance (Chap. 12)

The Book of Immanuel concludes with a song of trust (12:1-3) and a song of thanksgiving (12:4-6), two praise hymns that would be sung by the returning exiles. The last half of 12:2 quotes Exodus 15:2, part of a song that commemorated the Egyptian defeat at the Red Sea at the time of the Exodus. Isaiah 7 begins with war and terror (7:1-2), but Isaiah 12 ends with joy and praise.

THEMES FROM ISAIAH 7–12

The prophet was conscious of Judah's alienation from God. When speaking to King Ahaz, Isaiah referred to the Lord not as "our God" but as "my God" (Isa. 7:13), implying that Ahaz was merely giving lip service to his relationship to the Lord. Isaiah and the Lord both referred to Judah as "this people" or "these people" (8:5,11,12), not as "my people" or "our people." Judah's wickedness had erected barriers between the people and their God. Sin always destroys fellowship and leads to alienation.

The prophet was conscious of God's presence in his life. The Lord spoke to Isaiah again and again (7:3; 8:1,5,11), and the prophet knew that the strong hand of God was upon him (8:11). In a similar way, Ezekiel sensed the control of the Lord over his life (Ezek. 1:3; 37:1; 40:1). In the words of Brother Lawrence, who served as a cook in a Carmelite monastery in seventeenth-century France, every believer needs to learn "the practice of the presence of God."

The prophet was conscious of the future coming of the Messiah. Isaiah knew with full assurance that the "Wonderful Counselor," the "Mighty God," the "Everlasting Father," the "Prince of Peace" (Isa. 9:6), the "Branch" (11:1), the "Root of Jesse" (11:10) would some day come to rule the world in righteousness. The Messiah would also be called by the symbolic name "Immanuel" (7:14), which means "God is with us" (8:10). Many students of Scripture have observed that one of the most basic themes of the Bible is the Immanuel theme—God is with us. The Gospel of Matthew begins with the coming of Immanuel (Matt. 1:23) and ends with the Great Commission, which concludes with Jesus' words: "I will be with you" (28:20). The story of God's relationship with Moses begins with the Lord's statement to him, "I will be with you" (Exod. 3:12), and ends with the assertion that the Lord knew Moses "face to face" (Deut. 34:10). The Bible itself begins by describing a creation that centers on the formation of a human couple with whom God can have intimate fellowship (Gen. 1:26-27; 3:8-9) and ends with the words, "The grace of the Lord Jesus be with God's people" (Rev. 22:21). John Wesley, the founder of Methodism, summarized the significance of the Immanuel theme with his dying words, engraved on his tombstone in Westminster Abbey in London: "The best of all is this: God is with us."

For Study and Discussion

1. Where in the Old Testament can we find more examples of Israel's tendency to trust in her own military strength or political influene instead of in God? In what ways do we do this today?

2. Read Isaiah 7:12 and Deuteronomy 6:16. Give examples of how we also use Scripture in an attempt to justify our own willful natures.

3. What was the root of Ahaz's error? What possible reasons can you think of why he would be so completely disinterested in God's offer of a miraculous sign?

4. Look up the New Testament Scriptures that confirm the messianic prophecy of Isaiah 9:1-7. (Matt. 1:1; 3:13-17; 4:12-17; Luke 1:34-35,76-79; John 3:16; 14:9-10; Heb. 1:1–3.)

5. From Isaiah 10:5-9 what conclusions can be drawn about God's justice as it concerns the prosperity of wicked men?

Note
1. See R.C. Stedman, *Highlights of the Bible* (Ventura: Regal Books, 1981), pp. 85-87; G.L. Archer, *Decision*, December, 1976, pp. 6,12; G.L. Archer, "Isaiah," *The Wycliffe Bible Commentary* eds. C.F. Pfeiffer and E.F. Harrison (Chicago: Moody Press, 1962), p. 618.

5

ISAIAH'S NEIGHBORS

Isaiah 13—23

Although Isaiah's primary mission and message was the proclamation of the word of God to his own people, the people of Judah and Jerusalem, he was by no means narrow or provincial in his outlook. Like two other major prophets (Jer. 46–51; Ezek. 25–32) and two of the minor prophets (Amos 1–2; Zeph. 2:14-15), Isaiah included in his writings a section that demonstrates the international scope of the prophetic vision (Isa. 13–23). Called the Book of Oracles Against the Nations, it is the second of the seven basic literary units into which we have divided the prophecy of Isaiah. For the most part it is concerned with foreign nations; but the oracle concerning Judah in Isaiah 22 reminds us that Israel's God played no favorites and that He judged sin no matter who committed it.

BABYLON (Isa. 13:1—14:27; 21:1-10)

Ten nations in all are treated in Isaiah 13–23. The oracle against Babylon (see also Jer. 50–51) is not only first on the list (13:1—14:27) but is also supplemented later as well (21:1-10). During the time of Isaiah, Babylon was still part of the Assyrian empire (14:25), which posed a serious threat to Judah's existence during Isaiah's entire ministry. Furthermore, the Babylonians under Nebuchadnezzar would destroy Judah and Jerusalem between 605 and 586 B.C. It is understandable, then, that Isaiah devoted considerable space to the Assyro-Babylonian menace and pronounced God's judgment on the rulers and people of those lands.

The Hebrew word for "oracle" appears ten times throughout Isaiah 13–23 (13:1; 14:28; 15:1; 17:1; 19:1; 21:1,11,13; 22:1; 23:1). It is related to a Hebrew verb meaning "lift up, carry," and it refers either to lifting up one's voice or carrying a burden. It usually implies a pronouncement of doom when used in reference to the nations.

In Isaiah 13 the prophet predicted that Babylon and her people would be "overthrown by God" (13:19). The Lord "Almighty" was mustering an "army" for war (13:4; the Hebrew word for "Almighty" is the plural of the word for "army"). The day of judgment would come against Babylon like "destruction" from the "Almighty" (13:6; the Hebrew word for "Almighty"—different from the one in 13:4—sounds like the word for "destruction"). The Medes (13:17) would join the Babylonians in defeating Assyria in 612-609 B.C., but later they would ally themselves with the Elamites (21:2) and Persians under the leadership of Cyrus (45:1) to conquer Babylon in 539 B.C. (47:1). The Lord would use the armies of Babylon's neighbors to judge her arrogance and pride (13:11). The women and children of Babylon would suffer terribly (13:16), a reminder to us that the ravages of war often affect innocent and helpless people most severely (2 Kings 8:12; Ps. 137:8-9; Hos. 10:14; Amos

1:13; Nah. 3:10; Zech. 14:2).

The account of the conquest of Babylon is painted on a broad canvas. Its backdrop is "the day of the LORD" (Isa. 13:6,9), a time not only of judgment on the nations but also of restoration for Israel (14:1-3). Capable of more than one fulfillment throughout human history, the day of the Lord is characterized by darkness (13:11; Joel 2:10,31; Amos 5:18,20; Zeph. 1:15; Rev. 6:12-13) and desolation. It is indeed the day of the Lord's wrath (Isa. 13:5,9,13; Zeph. 1:15,18).

In its heyday during the reign of Nebuchadnezzar (605-562 B.C.), the city of Babylon would become "the jewel of kingdoms" (Isa. 13:19). The hanging gardens, planted by Nebuchadnezzar for his Median wife, would be known far and wide as one of the seven wonders of the ancient world. But the king's arrogance (Dan. 4:28-30) would prove to be his own undoing. He would be humbled by the Lord (Dan. 4:31-33), and within a generation of his death the Babylonian kingdom would be no more (5:30). Babylon would fall, and her gods would fall with her (Isa. 21:9). Her southernmost territory, so carefully tilled and irrigated throughout the centuries, would revert to swampland (14:23), and by the seventh century A.D. Babylon would be completely deserted (13:20).

Isaiah 14:4-23 consists of a taunt-song against the king of Babylon, a poem that heaps scorn and ridicule upon him. The nations he oppressed break into singing (14:4-7), and nature itself rejoices at his fall (14:8). The spirits of deceased kings are pictured symbolically as greeting him when he arrives in the netherworld (14:9-10), and they ponder his fate as they stare at him (14:16-17). Ultimately his corpse is thrown from his tomb and trampled underfoot (14:19-20).

Ever since the days of Tertullian, one of the early Church fathers, various students of Scripture have interpreted Isaiah 14:12-15 as referring to the fall of Satan. The Latin Vulgate translation, followed by the King James Version, rendered "morning star" (14:12) as "Lucifer" (which means "light-bearer"), a name subsequently and popularly applied to the Devil. Jesus' statement in Luke 10:18, "I saw Satan fall like lightning from heaven," is often cited as a parallel to Isaiah 14:12, which speaks of someone as having "fallen from heaven."

But, however attractive such an interpretation might appear at first, the entire context surrounding Isaiah 14:12-15 pertains to an unnamed "king of Babylon" (14:4). He has "subdued nations" (14:6), he has "become like" other kings (14:10), he is in the grave where "worms cover" him (14:11), he is referred to as a "man" (14:16-17). At the same time he uses high-flown language as his claims to be divine (14:13-14), a common practice among the kings of Babylon and Assyria, who often considered themselves to be gods worthy of worship.[1]

It is also true, however, that beginning in the days of the tower of Babel (Gen. 11:1-9) the name *Babylon* has been applied to political and religious systems opposed to the living God. The king of Babylon in Isaiah 14 embodied satanic power, and he may very well be a prefiguration of the "beast" who will be worshiped (Rev. 13:4) by many and will be associated with the "Babylon" of the last days (Rev. 17:3-5). Jesus' vision of Satan's fall resulted from the successful evangelistic campaign of seventy-two of His followers, who reported that "even the demons" submitted to commands uttered in Jesus' name (Luke 10:17). The fall of the king of Babylon (Isa. 14:12) is matched by the fall of Babylon herself (21:9), whose ruins in the last days are pictured as a "home for demons" (Rev. 18:2). The sovereign might of the Lord always overwhelms the demonic powers of Babylon, whether earthly or heavenly.

PHILISTIA (Isa. 14:28-32)

Isaiah's oracle against the Philistines is dated precisely (14:28) "in the year King Ahaz died" (715 B.C.). Although King David had soundly defeated the Philistines in the early years of his reign (2 Sam. 5:17-25), descendants of the survivors continued to inhabit their coastal plain for centuries. Eventually their name in modified form—*Palestine*—was given to the entire land of Canaan. During Isaiah's time the Philistines were still strong enough to go to war against Ahaz (2 Chron. 28:16-18) and Hezekiah (2 Kings 18:5-8). Philistia would be invaded by the Assyrians from the north (Isa. 14:31), but the Lord would protect Jerusalem (14:32). Several prophets (in addition to Isaiah) pronounced divine judgment on the Philistines (Jer. 47; Ezek. 25:15-17; Amos 1:6-8; Zeph. 2:4-7).

MOAB (Isa. 15—16)

Abraham's nephew Lot was the father of the original ancestor of the Moabites through an incestuous relationship with his own daughter (Gen. 19:36-37). Located east of the Dead Sea, Moab was an enemy of Israel throughout her history (Isa. 25:10; Num. 22:1-6; 2 Kings 13:20). Isaiah's oracle against the Moabites (see also Jer. 48; Ezek. 25:8-11; Amos 2:1-3; Zeph. 2:8-11) perhaps foresaw an invasion by King Sargon of Assyria in either 715 or 713 B.C. Assyria is called a "lion" (the traditional symbol of the Assyrian rulers) in Isaiah 15:9 (see also 5:29; Jer. 50:17) and "the destroyer" in Isaiah 16:4 (see also 33:1).

Isaiah predicted that the cities and villages of Moab would soon be "ruined" (15:1), and he listed many of them by name throughout his oracle. An important inscription by King Mesha (2 Kings 3:4) of Moab was found among the ruins of ancient Dibon (Isa. 15:2) in 1868, perhaps indicating that Dibon was Moab's capital during the days of the Israelite monarchy. Dibon is called "Dimon" in 15:9, punning on the Hebrew word for "blood" (*dam*) in the same verse.

Like the other nations in Isaiah's oracles, Moab had her own god—in this case, Chemosh (1 Kings 11:33). The Moabites worshiped him at their "high places" (Isa. 15:2; 16:12), which were shrines originally built on hilltops and usually associated with paganism. (1 Kings 11:7). But Chemosh, a mere idol (Isa. 44:17-20), was no match for the Lord (Isa. 16:12) and would soon look on helplessly as his worshipers were being destroyed by the enemy (16:13-14).

ARAM (Isa. 17)

Damascus (17:1), the capital of modern Syria, was also the capital of ancient Aram (which included roughly the same territory as Syria does today). From the time of King David and onward, the Arameans of Damascus were often at war with Israel (2 Sam. 8:5; 1 Kings 22:31). But during the days of King Ahaz they allied themselves with the northern kingdom of Israel (also known as Ephraim) and attacked Jerusalem, the capital of Judah (Isa. 7:1-2), as we noted earlier. Therefore Isaiah's oracle against Damascus (see also Jer. 49:23-27; Amos 1:3-5) singled out Ephraim for judgment as well (Isa. 17:3).

Isaiah predicted that Damascus would become "a heap of ruins" (17:1), and his prophecy was fulfilled in 732 B.C. when Tiglath-Pileser III captured the city and turned it into an Assyrian province. Many of Ephraim's cities suffered during the same invasion because their people had forgotten the Lord (17:10). The Assyrians—portrayed as "flood waters" (8:7) and as a "raging sea" (17:12)—would then "sweep on into Judah" (8:8), to the very gates of Jerusalem itself in the days of Sennacherib in 701 B.C. But in a single day the Lord would give the people of Jerusalem a reprieve and protect the holy city (17:14; 37:36-37).

CUSH (Isa. 18)

Chapters 18–20 of Isaiah form a trilogy: Isaiah 18 concerns Cush, 19 is an oracle about Egypt, and 20 is a prophecy against both Egypt and Cush. Early in Isaiah's ministry the rulers of Cush (the upper Nile region, roughly equivalent to modern Sudan) invaded Egypt and controlled it for about seventy-five years (about 730 to about 655 B.C.). Their domination came to an end as a result of intense military campaigns waged by the Assyrian rulers Esarhaddon and Ashurbanipal. Isaiah foresaw not only the coming destruction of Cush (18:5-6; see also, from a later period, Zeph. 2:12) but also that some day in the future the Cushites would bring gifts to the Lord in Jerusalem (Isa. 18:7; see also Ps. 68:31).

EGYPT (Isa. 19–20)

Isaiah's oracle against Egypt (see also Jer. 46; Ezek. 29–32) is half poetry (19:1-15) and half prose (19:16–20:6). As the Lord had brought judgment on "all the gods of Egypt" in the days of Moses (Exod. 12:12), so "the idols of Egypt" would soon tremble in the presence of God (Isa. 19:1). Internal strife would sap the people's energy as the Egyptians fought among themselves as well as against Cushites and

Libyans (19:2). Eventually a "cruel master" (19:4)—an Assyrian king—would overpower them: Esarhaddon would conquer them in 670 B.C., and Ashurbanipal would destroy their beautiful southern capital, the city of Thebes, in 663 (Nah. 3:8-10). Zoan, the northern capital, would have problems of a different sort. Although Egypt had a long tradition of being a fountainhead of wisdom (1 Kings 4:30), the officials of Zoan had become "fools" (Isa. 19:11,13).

But at some time in the future Egypt will pay homage to the Lord (19:18), acknowledge Him as their God, and worsip Him with sacrifices (19:21). In fact—wonder of wonders!—the Egyptians and the Assyrians, who had been mortal enemies for centuries, will some day worship the Lord together (19:23). Israel will join them in fulfilling the Abrahamic promise of blessing (19:24; see Gen. 12:3), and God will refer to Egypt as "my people" (Isa. 19:25; see also 45:14).

In the meantime, however, Egypt and Assyria continued their military adventures against each other (20:4). During Isaiah's ministry Philistia was often within Assyria's sphere of influence, and in 713 B.C. Ashdod, one of the five main Philistine cities (see 1 Sam. 6:17), rebelled against King Sargon II. In 711 Sargon sent his supreme commander to capture the city (Isa. 20:1), and because Egypt had participated in the rebellion the Assyrians humiliated them as well (20:4).

Because Sargon's name appears in the Bible only in Isaiah 20:1, it is understandable that scholars of previous generations sometimes assumed that "Sargon" was another name for Shalmaneser V (727–722 B.C.) or for Sennacherib (705–681). But archaeological research over the past century or so has unearthed inscriptions that testify to the exis-

tence of not one Sargon but two: Sargon I (the Great),
who founded the dynasty of Akkad (see Gen. 10:10)
and ruled over southern Mesopotamia from about
2334 to about 2279 B.C., and Sargon II (722–705),
who occupied the throne of Assyria between the
reigns of Shalmaneser V and Sennacherib. An especially important excavation took place in 1963, when
archaeologists working at Ashdod (see Isa. 20:1)
uncovered three fragments of an Assyrian monument
commemorating Sargon's victory there and mention-
ing him by name.

EDOM (Isa. 21:11-12)

Since the older brother of Jacob (Israel) was Esau
(Edom; see Gen. 25:29-30), and since Edomites frequently invaded Israel and Judah in ancient times, it
is not surprising that Isaiah included Edom in his
oracles against the nations (see also 34:5-15; Jer.
49:7-22; Ezek. 25:12-15; Amos 1:11-12). "Seir" (Isa.
21:11) was another synonym for Edom (see Gen.
32:3), which was located south of the Dead Sea. The
word *Dumah* (Isa. 21:11), a pun on "Edom," means
"stillness" in Hebrew and is an ominous reference to
the deathly silence (see Ps. 94:17; 115:17) that would
hang over Edom following its destruction.

ARABIA (Isa. 21:13-17)

When the Assyrians destroyed Damascus in 732
B.C., the Bedouin Arabs in the nearby deserts were
affected as well. The Babylonians under Nebuchadnezzar would some day defeat the Arabs, including
the people of Dedan, Tema (Jer. 25:23-24; see Isa.
21:13-14) and Kedar (Jer. 49:28-29; see Isa. 21:16-
17). The simple weapons of the Arabs were totally
ineffective against the swords and bows (21:15) of
the Assyrians and, later, the Babylonians.

JUDAH (Isa. 22)

Because God judges sin no matter who commits it, Isaiah included the chosen people in his oracles against the nations (22:8,21), focusing his attention on the capital city of Jerusalem. One of the "choicest valleys" (22:7) around the city, probably either the Kidron to the east (see John 18:1) or the Hinnom to the south and west (see Josh. 15:8), was the "Valley of Vision" in Isaiah's oracle (Isa. 22:1,5), the valley where God revealed Himself to the prophet in a vision.

Isaiah 22 is divided into two parts, the first (22:1-14) relating to the city as a whole and the second (22:15-25) concerned with one of the palace officials. Anticipating Sennacherib's attack on Jerusalem, King Hezekiah checked the royal arsenals, strengthened the city walls, and made a pool and tunnel to insure the city's water supply (2 Chron. 32:2-5; 2 Kings 20:20; see Isa. 22:8-11). Jerusalem's most important defenses, however, proved to be the praying king (Isa. 37:14-20) and the fearless prophet (37:21-32). Sennacherib failed to capture the city, lost his army and was forced to return to Assyria (37:33-37).

But the citizens of Jerusalem were slow to learn the lesson that the Lord blesses those who repent and judges those who sin. Forgetting that God had saved them from Sennacherib, they turned their beautiful city into a place of "tumult and revelry" (22:2,12-13) and set in motion the inevitable response of divine retribution (22:14). Nebuchadnezzar, God's agent of destruction (Jer. 25:9), would conquer Jerusalem in 586 B.C. Many of its inhabitants would die through disease and famine (2 Kings 25:3; see Isa. 22:2), and King Zedekiah and his army would flee the city, only to be captured near Jericho (2 Kings 25:4-6; see Isa.

22:3). The survivors of the Babylonian onslaught would weep over the fall of Jerusalem (Lam. 2:11) and refuse to be comforted (Isa. 22:4).

In the second half of his oracle against Judah, Isaiah turned his attention to Shebna, the palace administrator in Jerusalem (22:15) early in Hezekiah's reign. Shebna had cut out a tomb for himself in the rocky heights outside the city (22:16). Because such tombs were normally reserved for members of the nobility, Isaiah rebuked Shebna (22:17-19) and told him that he would be replaced by a man named Eliakim (22:20-24). Isaiah's prophecy was fulfilled when Eliakim became the palace administrator and Shebna was demoted to the position of secretary (37:2). Some scholars believe that the lintel of the very tomb that Shebna prepared for himself has been found by archaeologists.[2]

The office of palace administrator was second only to the king himself (see 2 Kings 15:5). He possessed the master key to the entire palace compound, and it was said of him that "what he opens no one can shut, and what he shuts no one can open" (Isa. 22:22). How sad then that Eliakim—like Shebna—eventually fell from power because of his own rebellious ways (22:25)! And how glorious to know that there is One who is "faithful as a son over God's house" (Heb. 3:6), who has "all authority in heaven and on earth" (Matt. 28:18), and who fulfills completely what Shebna and Eliakim could at best manage only partially—for it is said of Jesus that "what he opens, no one can shut; and what he shuts, no one can open" (Rev. 3:7)!

PHOENICIA (Isa. 23)

Although Isaiah's final oracle against the nations concerned Phoenicia as a whole (23:11), once again he focused his attention on the main cities that were the source of the nation's problems. Phoenicia was a commercial power that established colonies far and wide. Sidon (23:2,4,12; see also Ezek. 28:20-26) was one of its most prominent cities, and Isaiah predicted its destruction (Isa. 23:12)—fulfilled when it was captured by the Assyrian king Esarhaddon in the seventh century B.C. and also later by the Babylonian king Nebuchadnezzar about 587 (see Jer. 25:22).

But Isaiah placed his major emphasis on Tyre (see also Ezek. 26:1–28:19; Amos 1:9-10), the most important city in Phoenicia. Founded before 2000 B.C., it was an "old, old city" (Isa. 23:7) built partly on the Phoenician coast (23:1) and partly on two islands about a half mile from the shore (23:2,6). Isaiah compared Tyre's profiteering ways to those of a prostitute who tries to make the most money possible no matter what it take to do so (23:15-18). Because of Tyre's sin, Isaiah prophesied that divine judgment would overtake her (23:1,8-9). Nebuchadnezzar captured the mainland city in 572 B.C. (see Ezek. 26:7-11), and Alexander the Great destroyed the island fortress in 332 (see Ezek. 26:3-5). Tyre could no more escape God's wrath than could the other nine nations mentioned in Isaiah's oracles.

THEMES FROM ISAIAH 13–23)

Isaiah called every nation by name. Although poetic license led him to introduce a few of them by using a descriptive phrase ("the Desert by the Sea," 21:1; "the Valley of Vision," 22:1), he quickly identified them to avoid any possibility of misunderstanding ("Babylon," 21:9; "Judah," 22:8). God's judgments point toward a specific target, not a general horizon.

Isaiah knew each nation intimately. He was

familiar with the haughty pride of Moab (16:6), the feared aggressiveness of the Cushites (18:2,7), the self-assured confidence of Egypt's counselors (19:11), the carefree debauchery of Babylon (21:5), the voracious commercial appetite of Tyre (23:2,15-16). And by sad personal experience he was also familiar with the despairing indifference of his own beloved Jerusalem, whose people said, "Let us eat and drink, . . . for tomorrow we die!" (22:13). Such is always the unthinking advice of all who have lost faith in God's power to save (1 Cor. 15:32).

Isaiah knew that each nation was doomed. Their people had sinned beyond the point of no return, their repentance was not anticipated, and Isaiah pronounced divine judgment on all of them— including Israel and Judah.

All of the nations would be judged within history, not beyond it. Although final judgment will take place at the time of events associated with the second coming of Christ, every nation can expect its sins to be judged by God during its own historical lifetime. Only when divine punishment is swift and sure does the world understand that "the wages of sin is death" (Rom. 6:23).

God's judgment is evenhanded. His justice plays no favorites: He punishes His chosen people and others with equal severity when their sins display equal rebellion. In fact, it is an unswerving principle of divine justice that judgment begins "with the family of God" (1 Pet. 4:17).

For Study or Discussion

1. What is meant by "the day of the LORD?" (Isaiah 13:6,9)

2. Exactly how did God humble the king of Babylon to fulfill the prophecy o Isaiah 14:4-20? Who was this king? Would the words of Nebuchadnezzar in Daniel 4:34-36 indicate that Isaiah's prophecy was aimed not at Nebuchadnezzar but at his successor Belshazzar?

3. What support in Scripture can be found for the idea that the "Babylon" in Isaiah 14 refers not to the literal city, but rather to nations or systems that oppose God in all ages? (Revelation 17:3-5)

4. Compare Isaiah 22:13 with Ecclesiastes 8:15. In what ways do these passagess differ?

5. Read Jonah 3:9-10. Could the nations mentioned by Isaiah in chapters 13–25 have repented and been spared as Nineveh was? If not, why not?

Notes

1. A Leo Oppenheim, *Ancient Mesopotamia* (Chicago: University of Chicago Press, 1964), pp. 98-99.
2. D.J. Wiseman, *Illustrations from Biblical Archaeology* (London: Tyndale Press, 1958), pp. 59-60.

6

ISAIAH'S APOCALYPSE

Isaiah 24—27

In the Book of Immanuel (1–12), the first of the seven basic literary units in Isaiah, the prophet is concerned largely with his own people: the citizens of Jerusalem and the inhabitants of Judah. In the Book of Oracles Against the Nations (13–23), the second unit, he widens his perspective to consider God's purposes for the surrounding countries. And now, in the Book of Apocalyptic Oracles (24–27), the third unit, the prophet's vision expands even further as he looks at the ways in which the will of the Lord is fulfilled throughout the entire world. Isaiah 24–27, then, forms a fitting conclusion to Isaiah 1–23.

The last book of the New Testament is sometimes called the "Apocalypse," which comes from a Greek word meaning "revelation." An apocalypse, however, is a prophetic revelation in a special sense: The inspired writer looks far into the future and watches in amazement as the Lord brings history to its spectacular finish. Although the book of Revelation is the best-known apocalyptic section in the Bible, others include parts of Daniel, Joel, Zechariah and Matthew. Last but not least is Isaiah 24–27, which scholars often refer to as the "Little Apocalypse." These four brief chapters contain alternating descriptions of judgment and restoration in the last days as God proves Himself victorious over the forces of evil.

JUDGMENT (Isa. 24)

Up to this point, judgment had been predicted for Judah and her neighbors. In 24:1, however, Isaiah prophesied that the Lord would devastate the whole world (see also 24:3-6,11,13,17-21). As God had scattered sinful mankind at the beginning of history (Gen. 11:9), so also He would scatter them at its end (Isa. 24:1). No elements of society would escape (24:2), and the catastrophe would be universal (24:3).

The final judgment was inevitable and irreversible because the people's sin had crossed the line of no return. Isaiah 24:5 has an ominously contemporary ring to it: "The earth is defiled by its people," but the pollution about which the prophet spoke was primarily spiritual and was caused by human violation of divine law. Although everlasting from God's standpoint, His covenant had been "broken" (24:5) by sinful mankind. In Isaiah's vision he saw a world that was almost completely depopulated (24:6), an earth in which music and merriment had virtually ceased (24:7-9).

In each of the four chapters of Isaiah's apocalypse the prophet made reference to a city that lay in ruins (24:10; 25:2; 26:5; 27:10). He probably intended it to represent a composite of various cities that were opposed to God at different times in history—cities like Babylon, Nineveh, Tyre, and Jerusalem itself. The wickedness of the city, which attracted to itself the most flagrant of sinners and the most violent of criminals, was a microcosm of the world, and both would fall under the wrath of divine judgment (24:12-13). A redeemed remnant of the people would survive and give glory to the Lord from the west (24:14) and from the east (24:15)—indeed, from the ends of the earth (24:16)—but they would be "very few" in number (24:6).

For a brief moment Isaiah returned to his own historical situation and his personal involvement in it (24:16) as he reflected on his earlier response to his vision of God's glory: "Woe to me" (6:5). The coming apocalypse reminded him temporarily of the treachery of the Assyrians in the days of Ahaz and Hezekiah (24:16; see 33:1).

But his mind quickly reverted to the awesome scene spreading out before him, and he described it in powerful and memorable language that would be quoted later by another prophet: The earth's people would be seized by "terror and pit and snare" (24:17-18; Jer. 48:43-44). The series of Hebrew words so translated forms an outstanding example of alliteration and assonance: *pakhad* (pronounced PAH-khahd) and *pakhat* (pronounced PAH-khaht) and *pakh* (pronounced PAHKH). No sinner will be able to escape God's judgment on the day of the Lord. If anyone flees the sound of terror, he will fall into a pit; if he climbs out of the pit, he will be caught in a snare. Amos 5:19 describes judgment day in a similar way. If a sinner fled from a lion, he would meet a bear; if he ran into his house to escape the bear, a snake would bite him. "Out of the frying pan, into the fire," we would say. Divine retribution on the day of the Lord is inevitable.

Isaiah foresaw that the floodgates of the heavens will be opened (Isa. 24:18), as in the days of Noah (Gen. 7:11). Earthquakes will split the earth open, causing it to stagger and fall like a drunkard—"never to rise again" (Isa. 24:19-20). And all of this will take place "in that day" (24:21; 27:1,12), an ominous shorthand expression referring to the judgment day of the Lord.

Rulers, both heavenly and earthly, will share the fate of the earth itself. The "powers in the heavens" (24:21) are the devil and his fallen angels, whom Paul describes as "spiritual forces of evil in the heavenly realms" (Eph. 6:12). It is Satan in particular who will be "shut up in prison" (Isa. 24:22), bound for a thousand years, locked and sealed in the "Abyss" (Rev. 20:2-3). After many days he and his followers will be punished (Isa. 24:22) by fire and by being "thrown into the lake of burning sulfur" (Rev. 20:9-10).

A scene of judgment rarely presents a pleasant picture, and this is no exception. But the day of the Lord will also usher in the new heavens and the new earth. If it is true that the sun and moon do not shine during times of judgment (Amos 5:18,20; Zeph. 2:15; Isa. 13:10), it is also true that there is no need for them to shine when the Lord Himself is the "everlasting light" (60:19-20) as He and His servants reign in splendor over the new Jerusalem (24:23; Rev. 21:23; 22:5).

RESTORATION (Isa. 25:1–27:6)

In joyful response to God's revelations of coming judgment both in Isaiah's own time and in the distant future, the prophet recorded four hymns of thanksgiving that emphasize the theme of restoration.

For the Salvation of the Nations (25:1-8)

Every city that represented imperial power would be destroyed (25:2) and their ruthless and cruel armies (25:4-5), which covered the earth like a shroud (25:7), would be annihilated. The nations that had been oppressed and conquered by them would join their praise (25:3) to that of Isaiah himself (25:1), and both would honor and exalt the Lord for His great deliverance. God can always be counted on to protect the poor and needy while at the same time opposing the aggressor (25:4-5).

Isaiah predicted that on Mount Zion in the last days the Lord would host a great "feast," a "banquet" (25:6), which reminds us of the coming "feast with Abraham, Isaac and Jacob in the kingdom of heaven" (Matt. 8:11) as well as of the "wedding supper of the Lamb" (Rev. 19:9). Because those days will be a time of life and laughter, the Lord will swallow up death and wipe away all tears (Isa. 25:8). Joy and celebration will take the place of shame and disgrace.

For Zion's Happiness and Moab's Humiliation (25:9-12)

The Lord's people, who lived on Mount Zion, were characterized by trust in Him, and therefore they would rejoice in the salvation His grace would bring them (25:9-10). By contrast the Moabites, who lived in walled fortresses, were characterized by pride (16:6; 25:11), and therefore they would suffer because of the destruction the Lord's judgment would bring on them (25:10-12). Just as Edom symbolizes all the enemies of God in 34:5-17, so also Moab represents God's enemies here. The principle is clear: All who trust in the Lord are saved, but all who trust in their own resources are judged.

For Judah's Restoration and Resurrection (26:1—27:1)

The third of Isaiah's hymns is by far the longest of

the four. Its first stanza (26:1-6) summarizes the message of the second hymn by pointing out that since God is the true Rock (26:4) and salvation is the only fortress that really matters (26:1), the only sensible thing to do is to trust in the Lord (26:4; 30:15). Such trust is never misplaced, because God promises "perfect peace" to all who depend on Him rather than on themselves or their fortification (26:3). The Hebrew phrase translated "perfect peace" means literally "peace, peace" and is repeated in 57:19, where the Lord promises peace and healing to His people. By contrast, the Lord would some day condemn false prophets and their mercenary activities: "They dress the wound of my people as though it were not serious. 'Peace, peace,' they say, when there is no peace" (Jer. 6:14; 8:11).

The second stanza (26:7-11) is divided into two equal halves, the Lord's relationship to the righteous forming the subject of the first half (26:7-9a) and His relationship to the wicked the subject of the second half (26:9b-11). The path of the righteous is level and smooth (26:7; 40:3-4) because they walk in accordance with God's laws (26:8), they desire to do His will, and they yearn to be in His presence (26:9). The wicked, on the other hand, learn righteousness only as a result of divine judgment (26:9). Even though prosperity is showered down on them (26:10; Matt. 5:45) they continue in their evil ways and are therefore ripe for destruction (Isa. 26:11).

Stanza three (26:12-15) emphasizes the twofold truth that God's enemies are punished and eventually forgotten (26:14) while God's people live in a nation that is enlarged and possess borders that are extended (26:15). The focus, however, is always on God's activity, not on that of the people themselves (26:12,15). Although other "lords" (like the kings of

Assyria and Egypt) had occasionally ruled over the people of God, His followers were determined to honor Him alone (26:13).

The fourth stanza (26:16-18) reflects the despondency of God's people when oppressed by foreign rulers (26:16). Although Abraham's descendants were destined to be "a light for the Gentiles" (42:6; 49:6) and a blessing to the whole earth (Gen. 12:3), up to this point in their history they had failed miserably (Isa. 26:18).

But stanza five (26:19) presents God's solution to Israel's inadequacy. Using the imagery of resurrection, Isaiah predicted the restoration of the people of Judah following the Babylonian exile in a manner similar to that of Ezekiel 37:11-12. Like Ezekiel, however, Isaiah provided a vision that would some day be fulfilled again, this time on a much higher level, when the bodies of the believing dead would rise from their graves and shout for joy. Paul adds that when that glorious event takes place "we will be with the Lord forever" (1 Thess. 4:17).

The sixth stanza (26:20-21) refers to that coming day of the Lord, a time when God's wrath would fall on the sinful nations of the world (Zeph. 1:15,18). From the standpoint of God's timetable, the Assyrian oppression and the Babylonian captivity would last only "a little while" (Isa. 26:20).

Like stanza five, the seventh and final stanza (27:1) consists of only one verse. But what a majestic climax to Isaiah's magnificent hymn! The prophet's eyes looked into the remote future and saw the ultimate destruction of Satan himself. The symbol used is that of the sea monster, Leviathan, who often appears as a vivid portrayal of wicked nations such as Egypt (see 51:9,; Ezek. 29:3; 32:2). But Leviathan (or Lotan, as the name may have also been pronounced) was called the "gliding serpent" and the "coiling serpent" in Canaanite religious texts as well as in Isaiah, and in those texts he was described as a creature having seven heads[1] (see also Ps. 74:14) and as the mortal enemy of various Canaanite deities. We are reminded that a "dragon with seven heads" (Rev. 12:3) is the "ancient serpent called the devil or Satan, who leads the whole world astray" (12:9). But just as the doom of the Canaanite Lotan was sealed, so also the Lord would some day destroy Leviathan (Isa. 27:1) when He would seize "the dragon, that ancient serpent, who is the devil, or Satan" (Rev. 20:2), and throw him into a "lake of burning sulfur" (20:10). The figurative language used in Isaiah 27:1 is striking indeed and was well suited to focus attention not only on the final defeat of Israel's ancient political enemies but also on the ultimate destruction of Satan in the last days.

For the Lord's Protection of His People (27:2-6)

Isaiah's fourth and final hymn of thanksgiving depicts Israel as a vineyard (27:2) and recalls an earlier vineyard song (5:1-7). But the hymn in Isaiah 27 differs greatly from the song in Isaiah 5. In the song the Lord said He was going to destroy His vineyard (5:5-6) because it had produced bad fruit (5:2,4), while in the hymn the Lord guards His vineyard "so that no one may harm it" (27:3). In the song the vineyard would become a wasteland where "briers and thorns" would thrive (5:6), while in the hymn the Lord would set on fire any "briers and thorns" that might confront Him (27:4). In the song the vineyard's fruit was condemned by the Lord because it was bad (5:4-5), while in the hymn Isaiah looked forward to the time when Israel's fruit would fill the world (27:6)—that is, when the "Branch of the LORD" (4:2), the "Root of Jesse" (11:10), the Messiah would come and "bear fruit" (11:1). And last but not least, in the song it is quite evident that the Lord is displeased with His vineyard (5:3-4), while in the hymn he says, "I am not angry" (27:4).

The song of the vineyard (5:1-7) teaches us that the Lord judged His chosen people because of their rebellion and disobedience. By contrast, Isaiah's final hymn of thanksgiving (27:2-6) teaches us that some day the Lord would shelter the faithful remnant of His people with His protecting hand (27:5).

JUDGMENT (Isa. 27:7-11)

After a lengthy section on judgment (chap. 24) and an even lengthier section on restoration (25:1–27:6), Isaiah concluded his Book of Apocalyptic Oracles with a brief section on judgment (27:7-11) and an even briefer section on restoration (27:12-13).

Although the Lord "struck down" (27:7) the Assyrian troops who surrounded Jerusalem in 701 B.C. (37:36), He had not yet "struck her"—that is, Jerusalem herself. But in 586 B.C. the city would be destroyed by the Babylonians, who would come like a hot "east wind" (27:8) from the desert (Jer. 4:11; Ezek. 19:12), and the people of Judah would be carried off into exile. Only when God's people repudiated the worship of foreign gods and smashed their idols would their guilt be atoned for (Isa. 27:9). In the meantime the Lord would deal with them in judgment and not in compassion, because they were a people devoid of spiritual understanding (27:11)— just as Isaiah had described them at the beginning of his prophecy (1:3).

RESTORATION (Isa. 27:12-13)

But judgment was not Isaiah's last word, and it

would not be God's final response to His people. After exile comes restoration. The Lord would "thresh" the Promised Land from the Euphrates River in the northeast to the Wadi el-Arish in the southwest, the boundaries promised to Abraham (Gen. 15:18) and fulfilled during the reign of Solomon (1 Kings 4:21; 8:65). God's threshing would separate Jews from Gentiles, and the Israelites would be "gathered up one by one" (Isa. 27:12). Just as a mighty trumpet blast will call the elect together at the second coming of Christ (Matt. 24:31; 1 Cor. 15:52; 1 Thess. 4:16), so also a trumpet would some day sound to bring the northern exiles from Assyria and the southern exiles from Egypt to worship the Lord together on Mount Zion in Jerusalem (Isa. 27:13).

THEMES FROM ISAIAH 24—27

The main points that Isaiah made in these four chapters of his prophecy tend to be characteristic of apocalyptic writing in general:

Divine history is cosmic in scope. God is not a tribal deity who is interested only in a relatively small group of people. The God of the Bible is the Lord of history on the grand scale. His concern extends to the whole world (24:1,3-6,11,13) and His judgment is universal (24:19-20), affecting beings both celestial and terrestrial (24:21). It is impossible to hide from God (Gen. 3:8-10; Ps. 139:7-12).

Human history is permeated by sin. Apocalyptic writers tended to be pessimistic concerning history, and the Lord taught the authors of the Bible's apocalyptic literature to be keen observers of sinful human nature. All people were alike—they were sinful and destined for judgment on the day of the Lord (Isa. 24:17-18). All cities were equally doomed, whether pagan cities or the Holy City itself (24:10; 25:2; 26:5;

27:10). The only hope for the world as a whole would be the coming messianic kingdom.

Divine history is divided into two ages. The kingdom of the world will someday become "the kingdom of our Lord and of his Christ" (Rev. 11:15), the messianic kingdom. We are now living in this present age, but we will some day inhabit the age to come (Eph. 1:21). Although the present age is evil, the coming age will be glorious in every respect. God will pour out judgment on unbelievers but send showers of grace and blessing on believers "in that day" (Isa. 24:21; 25:9; 26:1; 27:1,2,12,13).

Human souls are immortal, and human bodies will be resurrected. Paul tells us that Christ Jesus "has destroyed death and has brought life and immortality to light through the gospel" (2 Tim. 1:10). It was necessary for Jesus to do so, because the subject of the afterlife is shrouded in darkness throughout most of the Old Testament. Job 19:25-27 and Daniel 12:2 come to mind when we think of resurrection and immortality, but Old Testament texts such as these are rare indeed. We can be grateful to Isaiah, then, for including in his Little Apocalypse two important passages on the doctrine of resurrection from the dead.

The first is 25:8, which states that God "will swallow up death forever." Paul quoted this text in 1 Corinthians 15:54 and said that it would be fulfilled when "the perishable has been clothed with the imperishable, and the mortal with immortality." Although death and the grave and the earth have swallowed up their victims throughout the centuries (Num. 16:32; Prov. 1:12), the Lord will some day reverse that terrifying process and swallow up death itself.

The second text in Isaiah is 26:19, which states

that the dead will live, that their bodies will rise, that those who dwell in the dust will wake up and shout for joy, and that the earth will give birth to her dead. Three examples of resurrection from the dead had already occurred in Israel's history (1 Kings 17:17-24; 2 Kings 4:18-37; 13:21), but some day all of God's people will rise from the dead. Their dew will be "like the dew of the morning" (Isa. 26:19), a beautiful symbol of life and fruitfulness (Hos. 14:5). "The last enemy to be destroyed is death" (1 Cor. 15:26), and "in Christ all will be made alive" (15:22).

"Come, Lord Jesus" (Rev. 22:20).

For Study or Discussion

1. Which of the prophecies in chapters 24–27 that are of global scope have yet to be fulfilled?

2. If the holy city of Jerusalem was not exempt from judgment and destruction, can the Church in the twentieth century consider itself safe from the same kind of judgment?

3. Is it safe to assume that the "Abyss" of Revelation 20 is the same as the "dungeon" of Isaiah 24:22? How are they connected?

4. In what ways are New Testament ideas about the afterlife foreshadowed by Isaiah 25:8 and 26:19?

5. How does the hymn of Isaiah 27:2-6 differ from the vineyard song of 5:1-7? Why is there a shift in tone?

Note

1. James B. Pritchard, ed., *Ancient Near Eastern Texts Relating to the Old Testament* 2nd ed. (Princeton: Princeton University Press, 1955), pp. 137-138; Walter Beyerlin, ed., *Near Eastern Religious Texts Relating to the Old Testament* (Philadelphia: Westminster Press, 1978), p. 198.

7

ISAIAH'S WOES

Isaiah 28—33

We have now arrived at the halfway point in our study of the book of Isaiah. The Book of Woes (Isa. 28—33) is the fourth of Isaiah's seven basic literary units, and it ends with chapter 33 of Isaiah's sixty-six chapter prophecy. The main Dead Sea scroll of Isaiah displays a section break between chapters 33 and 34, indicating the likelihood that the book of Isaiah was divided into two equal parts from the most ancient times. The Book of Woes, then, lies at the very heart of Isaiah's prophecy, and it is therefore understandable that the inspired writers of the New Testament quoted from the opening chapters of Isaiah 28—33 on numerous occasions (as we shall see).

But why "woes," of all things? Why should Isaiah choose to treat such a gloomy subject right in the middle of his book?

We cannot, of course, answer such a question with absolute confidence and certainty—but we would do well to remind ourselves that the theme of judgment and woe was central to the Old Testament prophetic message. The eyes of the Lord "are too pure to look on evil" (Hab. 1:13), and from His heavenly throne He rains judgment on the wicked (Ps. 11:4-6). the prophets were called by God to warn His sinful people that failure to repent would guarantee the coming of divine wrath against them.

Isaiah 28–33, like 5:8-23, consists of a series of six woes. Although the prophet himself did not reveal to us the historical background of the Book of Woes, its contents are contemporary with the final years of King Ahaz and the first half of King Hezekiah's reign.

WOE TO THE LEADERS OF EPHRAIM AND JUDAH (Isa. 28)

Isaiah denounced Samaria (28:1-4), and the capital of the northern kingdom of Israel (also called Ephraim). It was a beautiful city built on a magnificent hilltop, and the prophet compared it to a "wreath," a "fading flower," "set on the head of a fertile valley" (28:1). But it was ripe for divine judgment (28:4) because of its proud and drunken rulers (28:1,3), and so in 722 B.C. the Lord would bring against it the king of Assyria, "one who is powerful and strong" (28:2). Although most of the citizens of Samaria would be killed or deported, the Lord Himself would be a "beautiful wreath" for the survivors who remained faithful to Him (28:5-6).

The leaders of the holy city of Jerusalem, the capital of the southern kingdom of Judah, were for the most part just as wicked as those of Samaria, and Isaiah therefore denounced them as well (28:7-22). They too were proud (28:14-15), and they too were drunkards (28:7-8). Jerusalem's priests and prophets should have been filled with the Spirit (Num. 11:29; see also Eph. 5:18) but instead they were "befuddled with wine" (Isa. 28:7), which was contrary to the Law of Moses (Lev. 10:9). In their drunken stupor they made fun of the prophet Isaiah, insisting that he was treating them like infants by addressing them in baby talk (Isa. 28:9-10).

So the prophet told them that if they would not listen to him, God Himself would speak to them through the "foreign lips and strange tongues" of the Assyrian invaders (28:11). Although the Lord had given them the land of Canaan, they had not responded to Him in love and obedience (28:12). He would therefore judge them by using the same words that they had accused Isaiah of speaking to them (28:13).

And nothing the leaders of Judah could do would delay the "destruction decreed against the whole land" (28:22). Whether their "covenant with death" (28:15,18) refers to consulting the dead (8:19) or to an ill-advised treaty with Egypt (30:1-2), the Assyrians would come like a flood and sweep them away (28:17-19). The Lord had tested His people with His standards of justice and righteousness (28:17), and they had not measured up to His demands. So He would judge them, just as He had defeated the Philistines at Mount Perazim (28:21; referred to by its other name, Baal Perazim, in 2 Sam. 5:20) and the Amorites in the Valley of Gibeon (Isa. 28:21; Josh. 10:10-12). Although those earlier battles had been against Israel's enemies, God's warfare in Isaiah's time was called "his strange work," "his alien task," because he was now fighting against Israel herself (Isa. 28:21).

But as in the case of Ephraim (28:5-6) so also in Judah the Lord would have a faithful remnant, and He Himself would be their "precious cornerstone" (28:16). The "overwhelming scourge" (28:15,18) of the Assyrian army would surround Jerusalem in 701 B.C., and although the city would be unprepared militarily or spiritually (28:20) God would save those who trusted in Him—not because of their merit but because of His grace.

Isaiah 28 concludes with an agricultural parable cast in the form of a wisdom poem (28:23-29). The first stanza (28:23-26) states that God teaches the farmer the right way to plow his fields and plant his crops—implying that therefore God Himself knows the best means of judging His people and then restoring them. The second stanza (28:27-29) affirms that threshing is meant to be productive rather than destructive—implying that the same is true when God punishes His people. The Lord, who is "wonderful in counsel" (28:29; compare the description of the Messiah as "Wonderful Counselor" in 9:6), judges His people not to destroy them but to encourage them to repent.

WOE TO JERUSALEM (Isa. 29:1-14)

Having denounced Samaria briefly and Jerusalem at length in Isaiah 28, the prophet next focused his attention on Jerusalem alone (29:8), "the city where David settled" (29:1; see 2 Sam. 5:6-9). The holy city is called "Ariel," a word of uncertain meaning, only here (Isa. 29:1,2,7). The Lord's fire was in Zion and His furnace was in Jerusalem (31:9), and the bloodshed of battle threatened to turn the city into a virtual "altar hearth" (29:2), the Hebrew word for which sounds like "Ariel" (similar Hebrew words for the same term appear in Ezek. 43:15-16). But the Hebrew word translated "altar hearth" may have been intended simply as a pun on "Ariel," because recent research on the proper name itself leads to the conclusion that it probably means "City of God"[1]—an appropriate title for Jerusalem (which is called "City of the Lord" in Isaiah 60:14).

Despite the people's meticulous observance of their religious festivals (29:1; 1:13-14) God would bring the Assyrians to attack their city, and her citizens would mourn and lament (29:2). The situation would become desperate, and the people of Jerusalem would hover between life and death (29:4). Then, when all hope seemed gone, the Lord would destroy the Assyrian army at the very gates of Jerusalem in 701 B.C. (29:5-6), and the enemy's dreams of victory would remain unfulfilled (29:7-8). The arrival of the Lord in His power and might (29:6) would be similar to that of the subsequent coming of the Messiah, who would assure Jerusalem's future redemption (Zech. 14:1-5).

But the futile dreams of the Assyrians were more than matched by the "deep sleep" of the people of Jerusalem (Isa. 29:10). Their hypocrisy and insincere worship (29:13) would result in divine judgment (29:14). They refused to listen to the words of God as delivered through prophet and seer (29:10), and they were equally determined not to read the words of God on a scroll (29:11-12). Ultimately, then, Jerusalem's doom was sealed—and the gracious divine rescue in 701 B.C. would be only a temporary reprieve.

WOE TO ALL WHO DENY GOD'S SOVEREIGNTY (Isa. 29:15-24)

Isaiah, on behalf of his people, confessed to the Lord that they were the clay and God was the potter (64:8). By contrast, the people turned things upside down by demanding the right to dictate the terms of the Creator's relationship to them (29:16). In their pride and arrogance the leaders of Jerusalem attempted to "hide their plans from the LORD" (29:15)— plans to form an alliance with Egypt against Assyria (30:1-2) during the reign of King Hezekiah.

But the Assyrians (symbolized by the trees of Lebanon in 29:17; see also 10:34) would in a "very short time" (29:17)—by 701 B.C.—be cut down, and the "fertile field" (the faithful remnant in Jerusalem) would thrive again. Even the deaf would hear the words of the scroll (29:18) that was a closed book to the wicked rulers in Jerusalem (29:11). Judgment would overtake the ruthless and the scoffers (29:20-21), while the humble and needy would find their joy in the Lord (29:19) and would worship the God of Israel (29:22-23).

FIRST WOE TO THE PRO-EGYPTIAN PARTY
(Isa. 30)

Throughout much of the history of the divided monarchy (931–586 B.C.), especially during its final century and a half, the rulers of Israel and Judah looked to Egypt for help against Assyria or Babylon. They often sent their ambassadors to Zoan (30:4)—ironic indeed, since their ancestors had served there as slaves (Ps. 78:12,43). One of the main responsibilities of the Old Testament prophets was to warn their fellow Israelites about the pitfalls of entering into alliances with foreign nations. So it is not surprising that Isaiah should deliver two strong denunciations against the rulers of Judah whose sympathies were pro-Egyptian (the first in Isa. 30, the second in Isa. 31–32).

Treaties with sinful and treacherous Egypt were not in accordance with God's plans (30:1). They originated in the obstinacy and rebellion of Judah's rulers (30:1,9,16). Egypt's help was useless (30:7) and would bring only shame and disgrace to Judah (30:3-5). The journey of Judah's envoys from Jerusalem to Egypt through the desert of the Negev (30:6), the hot dry wasteland south of Israel, would bring them only hardship and distress. As the sea monster Leviathan (27:1) often symbolized wicked nations such as Egypt, so also Rahab (not the same as the Rahab of Josh. 2) was a large marine animal, perhaps the crocodile, symbolic of Egypt's arrogance (Isa. 30:7; 51:9; Job 26:12; Ps. 87:4; 89:10).

Although Judah's leaders were unwilling to trust either in the Lord (Isa. 30:1) or in His prophets and seers (30:10), they were prepared to rely on all kinds of things that were unworthy of their trust: "pleasant things" and "illusions" (30:10), like the utterances of false prophets (1 Kings 22:13; Jer. 6:13-14; 8:10-11; 23:16-17,25-26); oppression and exploitation of their own people and deceit in their dealings with neighboring nations (Isa. 30:12); swift horses and other military expedients (30:16); and, of course, alliance with Egypt—whose help was "utterly useless" (30:7). Their refusal to repent of their sins and trust in the Lord for their salvation (30:15) brought upon them the fulfillment of the curse of Deuteronomy 32:30, where Moses declared that one enemy soldier would be able to put a thousand sinful Israelites to flight (see Isa. 30:17).

But a patient and merciful God wanted to be gracious and compassionate toward the believing remnant of His people (30:18). He did not want "anyone to perish, but everyone to come to repentance" (2 Pet. 3:9). He was prepared to answer as soon as they cried for help (Isa. 30:19). They needed only to turn from their idolatry and follow Him (30:22). Although He had punished them by forcing them to eat bread and drink water like a common prisoner (30:20; see 1 Kings 22:27), their sincere repentance would some day bring them rich and plentiful food (Isa. 30:23) as one aspect of the Lord's blessings to them (30:24-26).

As for the Assyrian invaders, God's wrath would be poured out on them (30:27-33) in judgment. The "Name of the LORD" (30:27), symbolizing His power and glory (59:19), would come in order to demonstrate God's personal interest in Assyria's destruction. The redeemed people of the Lord would celebrate as if on the day of the Passover festival (30:29; 31:5), and God's victory over Assyria would cause the women of Judah to sing and dance to the music of tambourines (30:32; see also Exod. 15:20-21; 1 Sam. 18:6). The Assyrian king would suffer a fate like that of being burned to death at Topheth (Isa. 30:33), a region outside Jerusalem where idolatrous people engaged in the horrible practice of sacrificing their children to Molech (2 Kings 23:10; Jer. 7:31-32; 19:5-6,11-14), the god of the Ammonites (1 Kings 11:7).

SECOND WOE TO THE PRO-EGYPTIAN PARTY (Isa. 31–32)

Isaiah 31 is a brief summary of Isaiah 30 (compare 31:1 with 30:1-2,16; 31:3 with 30:3,5; 31:4 with 30:27; 31:5 with 30:29; 31:6 with 30:9,19; 31:7 with 30:22; 31:8 with 30:32; 31:9 with 30:33), and its backdrop is the same as well: the deliverance of Jerusalem from the Assyrian army in 701 B.C. Judah was to trust in the Lord, not in Egypt (31:1,3), for redemption in the face of the Assyrian onslaught. The Lord would come down (31:4) and protect the holy city. As on the day of the tenth plague, the slaughter of the Egyptian firstborn, when the destroying angel "passed over" every Israelite house that had blood on the doorframe (Exod. 12:13,23), so also the angel of the Lord would destroy the Assyrian troops surrounding Jerusalem while at the same time He would "pass over" the city itself and save its inhabitants (Isa. 31:5; 37:35-36). A "sword, not of mortals" (31:8), would devour the Assyrians.

Although Isaiah 32 looks forward ultimately to the messianic age (see especially 32:1,15-17), the historical context is still the impending Assyrian invasion of 701 B.C. The women of Jerusalem were complacent (32:9), but their feelings of security would soon change to fear as the Assyrians advanced and stripped the bountiful fields around the city (32:10-13). Jerusalem would be temporarily spared, but some day she would be devastated (32:14) by the Babylonians (586 B.C.). Not until the Messiah came to pour out His Spirit on His people (32:15) would they enjoy genuine and permanent security (32:17-18). Only then would their material and spiritual needs be fully met (32:2-4,20).

WOE TO THE DESTROYER (Isa. 33)

The prophet's first five woes (Isa. 28–32) were addressed almost exclusively against the people of God, but the sixth was leveled against Assyria, the "destroyer" (33:1; see 16:4), the "traitor" (33:1; see 21:2; 24:16). The city of Jerusalem in the days of the Assyrian king Sennacherib was like a ship unprepared to sail into battle (33:23) and defend herself. So her people prayed to the Lord, asking Him to rescue them in their time of distress (33:2-9). Jerusalem's brave defenders felt helpless, and her "envoys of peace" (33:7) had failed in their discussions with the Assyrian field commander (36:2-22). Travel and commerce had become impossible (33:8), and the entire land—from Lebanon in the north to Sharon and Carmel in the west to Bashan in the east to the Arabah in the south—had been devastated by the invaders (33:9). Only the Lord could save His people from certain destruction (33:2-6).

And He, always faithful, promised to do so (33:10). The defeat of the Assyrians would be both complete and swift (33:12). Their officers, their arrogance, their strange language—all would soon be nothing but unpleasant memories (33:18-19). Although sinners in Jerusalem would suffer divine judgment (33:14), her righteous citizens would receive God's blessing (33:15-16). Their eyes would see both the king (33:17) and His city (33:20)—perhaps Hezekiah and the earthly Jerusalem as an initial fulfillment, but surely the Messiah and the heavenly Jerusalem as the ultimate glorious fulfillment, when God Himself would be the King (33:22), the Mighty One (33:21). The coming Messiah would heal His people's diseases and forgive their sins (33:24).

THEMES FROM ISAIAH (28—33)

As we pointed out at the beginning of this chapter, the New Testament quotes frequently from Isaiah 28 and 29. In so doing it gives us a number of important insights into the nature of the Lord's dealings with us.

God condemns hypocrisy. In Matthew 15:8-9; Mark 7:6-7 Jesus quoted Isaiah 29:13 in order to rebuke the Pharisees and teachers of the law who were nullifying the divine Word for the sake of their human traditions. Because the heart "is deceitful above all things and beyond cure" (Jer. 17:9), hypocrisy is an ever-present temptation. It is all too possible for us as well to honor God with our lips even when our hearts are far from Him.

God despises human wisdom. In 1 Corinthians 1:19 Paul quoted Isaiah 29:14 to stress the fact that "the foolishness of God is wiser than man's wisdom" (1 Cor. 1:25). In order to unmask the vaunting pride of so much of what passes for human wisdom, God has deliberately chosen the foolish and weak and lowly and despised things of the world through which to accomplish His perfect will (1:27-31). Divine wisdom of course is to be eagerly desired, as King Solomon understood full well (1 Kings 3:6-14) and as James also knew (Jas. 1:5). It is merely human wisdom that we are to avoid whenever eternal issues are at stake.

God hardens the hearts of those who persistently refuse Him. In Romans 11:8 Paul quoted part of Isaiah 29:10 to show that it is possible for people to reject God, over and over and over again, to the point where He confirms that rejection and stops speaking to them. To use the language of Paul earlier in the same epistle: God eventually gives wicked people over to their "sinful desires" (1:24), their "shameful lusts" (1:26), their "depraved" minds (1:28). When that terrible moment arrives, they "have no excuse" (2:1).

God sometimes uses unusual means to get our attention. In 1 Corinthians 14:21 Paul quoted part of Isaiah 28:11-12 as he developed his teaching concerning the practice of speaking in tongues. Although in context Isaiah was referring to the Assyrian language and Paul was not, the principle still holds: God will use an unknown tongue, if necessary, to get His message through to us. If a strange language can be used to capture the attention of an unbeliever so that he will place himself under the hearing of the gospel, God does not hesitate to employ it (1 Cor. 14:22).

God alone is sovereign. In Romans 9:20 Paul quoted part of Isaiah 29:16 in order to press home the point that God shares His sovereignty with no one. Whenever the pot wants to be the potter, serious problems are the result. The Lord always knows what is best for us, and we always get ourselves into trouble when we try to help Him rule the universe. At fearful cost the patriarch Job finally learned that lesson, and his response to the Lord was the only appropriate one: "I despise myself and repent in dust and ashes" (Job 42:6).

God alone is our true foundation. In 1 Peter 2:6 the apostle Peter quoted Isaiah 28:16 with reference to Christ. Just as the cornerstone is the most important part of the foundation that supports the house, so also is Jesus, the Son of God, the true basis of our faith and of His Church. If we build upon Him, we cannot fail. And as Paul assured us—also quoting Isaiah 28:16—the one who trusts in Jesus "will never be put to shame" (Rom. 9:33; 10:11).

For Study or Discussion

1. Why were the "woes" of Isaiah 28–33 often quoted by New Testament writers?

2. Read 2 Kings 19:14-19. What do you think the faithfulness of Hezekiah had to do with the reprieve described in Isaiah 29:5-8 and 2 Kings 19:35?

3. Why was God displeased with the worship practices of the people of Judah (29:13)?

4. In what ways do we try to dictate the terms of our relationship with God? See Isaiah 29:16.

5. What sort of illegitimate alliances do we make that could be compared with Judah's?

Note

1. Ronald Youngblood, "Ariel, 'City of God'," in *Essays on the Occasion of the Seventieth Anniversary of the Dropsie University (1909-1979)*, ed. Abraham I. Katsh and Leon Nemoy (Philadelphia: Dropsie University, 1979), pp. 457-462.

8

ISAIAH'S COUNSEL

Isaiah 34—39

The fifth of Isaiah's seven basic literary units is
the Book of Judgment and Restoration (Isa. 34—35),
and the sixth is the Book of Hezekiah (36—39). Isaiah
the prophet becomes Isaiah the counselor in these
two units, and his divinely inspired advice is especially noteworthy in chapters 36—39. The Book of
Hezekiah takes its name from the fact that King Hezekiah is prominent in each of its four chapters.
Isaiah 34—35 should therefore probably also be
assigned to his reign, particularly since chapters
28—33 are usually assumed to be from his time as
well.

THE BOOK OF JUDGMENT AND RESTORATION
(Isa. 34—35)

Just as chapters 24—27 are an apocalyptic section
that concludes chapters 1—23, so also Isaiah 34—35 is
a brief apocalyptic section that forms a fitting conclusion to chapters 28—33. As such, it has some of the
same apocalyptic features that characterize Isaiah
24—27 (the "Little Apocalypse").

Judgment on the Nations (Chap. 34)

Isaiah 34:1-4 depicts divine judgment on a cosmic scale. All the nations would be objects of God's wrath (34:2), which would consume them in the day of the Lord (13:13). Their destruction would be total (34:2), like the destruction of the Canaanites in the days of Joshua (Josh. 10:40). The stars would fall from the heavens, and the sky itself would be rolled up like a scroll (Isa. 34:4)—fulfilled ultimately at the second coming of Christ (Rev. 6:13-14).

The broad canvas of Isaiah 34:1-4 is reduced to postage-stamp size in 34:5-17, where the nation of Edom is chosen to represent and symbolize all of God's enemies (a function performed by Moab in 25:10-12). Although Edom (Esau) was the brother of Israel (Jacob; Obad. 8–10), the Edomites historically acted in anything but a brotherly manner toward the Israelites (Obad. 11–12; Ps. 137:7; Lam. 4:21-22). Therefore Edom would not escape the total destruction (Isa. 34:5) that had overwhelmed all the other nations (34:2). Edom was located south of the ruins of Sodom and Gomorrah, and the same kind of devastation that consumed those wicked cities would lay waste to the land of Edom as well (34:9; Gen. 19:24). Ceremonially unclean birds (Deut. 14:13-17) would haunt the remains of her once beautiful buildings (Isa. 34:11,15). So complete would be her destruction that it could be described as "chaos" and "desolation" (34:11)—the same two words translated respectively as "formless" and "empty" in Genesis 1:2. And all of this would happen because of Edom's relentless hostility toward Israel (Isa. 34:8; 63:1-6).

When was Isaiah's prediction about the destruction of Edom fulfilled? Not too long after the destruction of Jerusalem in 586 B.C., it would seem. Edom gloated over Jerusalem's fall (Ps. 137:7), but her own turn would come in the Lord's good time. Nabatean Arabs drove the Edomites from their homeland, possibly as early as 500 B.C. The first-century Jewish historian Josephus identified the Nabateans as descendants of Nebaioth, whose sister Mahalath was one of the wives of Esau/Edom (Gen. 28:9). Josephus also stated that the Nabateans ruled east of the Jordan River all the way from the Red Sea in the south to the Euphrates in the north, which explains how the Nabatean king Aretas IV could be exercising authority in Damascus in the days of the apostle Paul (2 Cor. 11:32). In New Testament times the territory formerly known as Edom was called Idumea (Mark 3:8), and it is ironic that Herod the Great, who tried to kill the baby Jesus, was an Idumean by birth. The enmity of Edom against Israel lasted till the bitter end.

Restoration of Israel (Chap. 35)

But if the doom of the Edomites was sealed by 500 B.C., Israel's greatest glory still lay in the future. The contrast between the horrors of Isaiah 34:5-17 and the matchless beauty and boundless rejoicing of chapter 35 is striking indeed. The slaughter in Edom's Bozrah (34:6) is hopelessly overshadowed by the splendor of Israel's mountains of Carmel and plains of Sharon (35:2). The same divine vengeance and retribution that would annihilate Edom (34:8) would save the people of God (35:4). Although Edom's desert would be populated with hyenas and wild goats and nameless creatures of the night (34:14), Israel's desert land would burst into bloom (35:1-2) and be watered by streams and springs (35:6-7). Even the princes of Edom would vanish (34:12), but Israel's weakest and most handicapped citizens would be strengthened and healed (35:3,5).

When would Isaiah's prediction about the restoration of Israel be fulfilled? The more immediate fulfillment would take place when the exiles, released from Babylonian captivity, would walk along the highway from Babylon to Jerusalem after being freed by the Persians under King Cyrus in 538 B.C. (35:8; 40:3-4,10-11; 44:28; 45:13). Having been redeemed from exile (35:9), the people of God would sing and rejoice as they marched into Jerusalem (35:10, a verse so important that it is repeated verbatim in 51:11).

But there would be a greater and more ultimate fulfillment of Isaiah 35 as well. The blind and the lame, the deaf and the mute (35:5-6) would find complete healing only with the arrival of the messianic age (Matt. 11:5; 12:22). Feeble hands would be strengthened and weak knees would be steadied (Isa. 35:3) only through the power released in the early Church by Christ (Heb. 12:12). Final restoration and redemption would be given to God's people only at the second coming of our Lord (Rom. 8:23).

With genuine longing we await that glorious day.

THE BOOK OF HEZEKIAH (Isa. 36—39)

With something of a jolt, the prophet Isaiah calls us back to the grim realities of his own situation. It was a critical time in the history of ancient Judah, and therefore the events are recorded more than once in the Old Testament. In fact, except for 38:9-20, Isaiah 36—39 is paralleled (sometimes verbatim) in 2 Kings 18:13—20:19. It would seem that the writer of 2 Kings made use of the prophecies of Isaiah as one of his sources.

Hezekiah and Sennacherib (Chaps. 36—37)

The "fourteenth year of King Hezekiah's reign"

(36:1) was 701 B.C., a year of crisis for the citizens of Jerusalem. The Assyrian king Sennacherib (705–681 B.C.) had invaded Judah because Hezekiah had rebelled against him (36:5) by refusing to make the expected annual payments of tribute (2 Kings 18:7). In his royal annals Sennacherib noted that he had captured forty-six cities of Judah. Included was the important city of Lachish (Isa. 36:2), located about thirty miles southwest of Jerusalem and stra- tegically situated to guard the main approaches to the holy city itself. But by 701 B.C. every garrison town protecting Jerusalem had been overrun by the Assyrian troops, and their field commander met with the city's main officials at a convenient place outside the walls to dictate terms of surrender to Hezekiah (36:2-4). Ironically, it was the very spot where Isaiah had confronted Hezekiah's father Ahaz more than thirty years earlier for a similarly critical meeting (7:3).

Hezekiah's officials pleaded with the Assyrian commander to speak to them in Aramaic (the diplo- matic language of that time) rather than in Hebrew, which the inhabitants of Jerusalem, some of whom were sitting atop the wall and listening in on the pro- ceedings, could of course understand (36:11). But the Assyrian refused to use Aramaic (36:13) because the things he had to say were intended for everyone in the city, not just for Hezekiah and his men (36:12).

The arguments of the field commander provide a fine example of ancient political diplomacy and psy- chology. He tried to demonstrate the supremacy of the king of Assyria by calling him the "great king" (36:4,13)—a title that was, however, regularly used by Assyrian monarchs. He belittled Egypt, a potential ally of Judah, by calling it a splintered reed that pierces the hand of anyone who leans on it (36:6; see also Ezek. 29:6-7). He falsely accused Hezekiah of engaging in activities that ridiculed the worship of the Lord (Isa. 36:7)—although Hezekiah had in fact destroyed shrines that had often been dedicated to the worship of Baal and other Canaanite deities (2 Kings 18:4; 2 Chron. 31:1). The Assyrian commander also made fun of the small size of Judah's army by offering to supply two thousand horses if Hezekiah could find enough men to ride on them (Isa. 36:8-9). Finally, the commander brazenly claimed that the Lord Himself had told him (or perhaps Sennacherib) to invade and destroy Judah (36:10).

After a brief interruption by Hezekiah's men (36:11) the Assyrian resumed his speech. Using crude language, he warned the population of Jerusalem of the horrors of the coming siege and of the suffering that would accompany it (36:12). He hammered away at the point that if they were wise they would pay attention to the king of Assyria (36:13) rather than to their own king (36:14,15,16,18). He insisted that Hezekiah was deceiving and misleading them by telling them to trust in the Lord, because no gods had ever been able to deliver their people from the power of Assyria's rulers (36:18-20). So the Assyrian field commander recommended surrender and the signing of a peace treaty as the only way to continued happiness and prosperity for the people of Judah (36:16-17).

The Assyrian hoped that his unassailable logic would undermine the people's morale and frighten them into submission. But Hezekiah (doubtless following Isaiah's advice) had commanded them not to respond in any way, and they obeyed him (36:21). It was the Lord Himself who would soon give the final answer to Sennacherib's troops because God, and not Sennacherib, is the only One worthy of the title "great King" (Ps. 47:2; 48:2; 95:3). In the meantime, however, Hezekiah's officials (Isa. 36:22)—and Hezekiah himself (37:1)—tore their clothes in an attitude of mourning. The situation seemed hopeless, and the leaders of Judah gave vent to their grief.

Hezekiah went to the Temple (37:1), which his ancestor Solomon had set aside as a place of prayer when it was originally dedicated to the service of the Lord (1 Kings 8:33). A godly king, Hezekiah sent word to the prophet Isaiah to join him in prayer on a day of "distress and rebuke and disgrace" (Isa. 37:2-4). Although most of Judah had already been devastated and many of its people killed, the king asked for prayer for "the remnant that still survives" (37:4).

Isaiah responded to Hezekiah's officials with a word of assurance ("Do not be afraid") and a divine prediction about Sennacherib ("I will have him cut down with the sword"). The Lord would calm the hearts of his own people (37:6) while at the same time compelling the Assyrian ruler to return to his homeland, where he would die (37:7). Shabataka, the new pharaoh of Egypt, had sent his brother Tirhakah (who later became pharaoh himself) with an army to help Judah repel the Assyrians (37:9). Sennacherib, when he learned this, reminded Hezekiah through messengers that nothing could help him now (37:10-13).

Knowing that he was powerless before the king of Assyria, Hezekiah turned to God for the strength he needed (37:14). His God was the only true King, "enthroned between the cherubim" (37:16) that adorned the ark of the covenant (1 Sam. 4:4). His God was the only true Sovereign, the only Creator of heaven and earth (Isa. 37:16). His God was the only living God, the only One who could hear and see and therefore answer (37:17), in contrast to the gods of

Assyria, who were "only wood and stone" (37:19). In short, Hezekiah's God was the only God worthy of the name, the only One who could deliver His people (37:20).

The earnest prayer of Hezekiah would soon be answered by the Lord (27:21). The prophet Isaiah brought God's word of assurance and victory to Judah's king (37:22-35). Like a virgin who preserves her chastity (37:22), Jerusalem would not be entered nor her walls broken through (37:33-34). Although the Assyrians had cut down Lebanon's tallest cedars (37:24), they would be unable to surmount Jerusalem's ramparts. Although neither desert lands nor the Nile river had slowed Sennacherib's military juggernaut (37:25), Jerusalem's God would prove to be more than he could handle. Although the Assyrians often led captives away by tying ropes to hooks placed in their noses (2 Chron. 33:11), they would soon receive the same treatment themselves (Isa. 37:29). Although the Assyrian field commander had promised abundant harvests to the people of Judah if they would only sue for peace (36:16-17), the Lord would provide them with everything they needed—and more beside (37:30-32). God had promised an everlasting throne to Hezekiah's ancestor David (2 Sam. 7:16; Isa. 9:7; 55:3), and therefore He would defend and save Jerusalem for David's sake as well as for His own (37:35).

The destruction of the Assyrians surrounding Jerusalem and the death of Sennacherib himself were not long in coming. Assyria's "large army" (36:2) met its untimely end when the angel of the Lord put 185 thousand soldiers to death (37:36). The Greek historian Herodotus, in recording his account of the event, says that mice or rats chewed through the leather fittings of the soldiers' weapons and made it necessary for them to beat a hasty retreat. But it may well be that Herodotus's rodents actually were carriers of a virulent disease—like septicemic plague, for example, which often causes its victims to become comatose and die within twenty-four hours.[1] An angel was sometimes sent by God to bring a deadly plague on sinful people (Exod. 12:12; 2 Sam. 24:15-16; 1 Chron. 21:22,27). In any event, the death of the Assyrian soldiers fulfilled Isaiah's earlier prophecies (Isa. 10:33-34; 30:31; 31:8).

Sennacherib, able to claim in his royal annals only that he made "Hezekiah, the Jew, . . . a prisoner in Jerusalem, his royal residence, like a bird in a cage," was forced to break camp and return to his capital city of Nineveh (37:37). Hezekiah had received new strength and life by going to the Temple of the Lord (37:1,14), but Sennacherib eventually met death while worshiping in the temple of his god Nisroch (37:38). He was assassinated in 681 B.C.—twenty years after his siege of Jerusalem—and succeeded by his son Esarhaddon (681–669). The Lord had warned that Sennacherib would be "cut down with the sword" (37:7), and his word is always fulfilled to the letter (37:38).

Hezekiah and Isaiah (Chap. 38)

Chapters 38–39 represent a flashback, since the events of 701 B.C. had not yet occurred (38:6) and the envoys of the Babylonian king Merodach-Baladan (who ruled 721-710 B.C. and again in 703) arrived after Hezekiah's recovery from illness (39:1). Just as chapters 36–37 fittingly conclude chapters 1–35, which have a strong Assyrian orientation, so also chapters 38–39 form a suitable introduction to chapters 40–66, which largely describe Judah's future relationships with the Babylonians.

Although Hezekiah and Isaiah were kindred spirits in various ways and in many settings, their relationship became especially close during the days of Hezekiah's nearly fatal illness (38:1). After the prophet announced to the king that he should put his house in order because he was going to die, Hezekiah wept and prayed to the Lord for mercy (38:2-3). Apparently Hezekiah had not yet fathered a son, and therefore the Davidic dynasty was in jeopardy. Through Isaiah, the Lord told Hezekiah that his prayer was answered and that fifteen years would be added to his life. How sad that Hezekiah's son Manasseh—born during those fifteen years—was to become the most wicked king ever to rule over Judah and was to be one of the major causes of the Babylonian exile (2 Kings 21:11-15)!

Whether the fact that "the sunlight went back" (Isa. 38:8) was caused by a temporary adjustment in the earth's rotation or involved the refraction of light we cannot say. But in gratitude for the Lord's goodness Hezekiah sang a hymn of thanksgiving (38:10-20) in two stanzas.

In the first stanza (38:10-14) the king voiced his complaint to the Lord. He had wanted to remain in "the land of the living" (38:11), not be forced to go through "the gates of death" (38:10) prematurely. He had been afraid that he would have to leave his body behind, like a tent (38:12; see also 2 Cor. 5:1,4; 2 Pet. 1:13-14). His suffering had brought forth the anguished cry: "O Lord, come to my aid" (Isa. 38:14).

In the second stanza (38:15-20) Hezekiah offered praise to God for His healing power. The king recognized that the disease and suffering had been for his ultimate benefit, and he also realized that his sin had been partially responsible (38:17). He was glad that he was still alive especially because knowledge about the afterlife was somewhat shadowy and uncertain during the Old Testament period (38:18)—in contrast to the light that Jesus and the gospel have shed on the subject (2 Tim. 1:10). Hezekiah's concluding promise (Isa. 38:20) reveals not only that he was a careful student of the psalms of his ancestor David (2 Chron. 29:30) but also that he shared David's interest in vocal and instrumental music (2 Sam. 23:1; Amos 6:5) as well as in the Temple (Ps. 23:6).

The prophet's instructions (Isa. 38:21) were probably directed to the court physicians, since the imperative verbs ("Prepare" and "apply") are plural. Figs were used as a remedy not only in Israel (38:21) but also farther north in the ancient town of Ugarit on the shores of Aram, as Canaanite inscriptions tell us. The sign that Hezekiah had requested (38:22) was probably the healing of the boil mentioned in 38:21. God had honored the king's prayer for physical restoration.

Hezekiah and Merodach-Baladan (Chap. 39)

The first half of Merodach-Baladan's name was the name of the chief Babylonian god, spelled "Marduk" by the Babylonians themselves. The king of Babylon "sent Hezekiah letters and a gift" (39:1), perhaps to enlist Hezekiah's support against the Assyrians. Judah's king made the mistake of escorting the Babylonian envoys on an ill-advised tour of his storehouses, including the armory (39:2). Although Hezekiah may have been requesting help from the Babylonians against the imminent Assyrian threat from Sennacherib, the information they gained from their careful inspection of Hezekiah's wealth and weapons would some day prove to be valuable indeed to Merodach-Baladan's powerful successors.

As Isaiah had confronted King Ahaz earlier (7:3),

so now he had to confront King Hezekiah and warn him that the Babylonians would some day plunder the royal palace in Jerusalem (39:3-6). Nebuchadnezzar of Babylon would carry off Hezekiah's own flesh and blood, and choice young noblemen like Daniel would become court servants (605 B.C.) in that faraway land (39:7; Dan. 1:3-6).

Isaiah 39 ends on a sad note. Apparently in submission to God's will, Hezekiah agreed that the Lord's word through Isaiah was good. Even as he spoke, however, he was thinking that at least there would be peace and security during his own lifetime (39:8). While it is true that he himself died a natural death as far as we know, his naive actions during the visit of the Babylonian envoys would bear bitter fruit in the lives of his descendants.

THEMES FROM ISAIAH 34—39

Two matters, in particular, stand out in these transitional chapters.

God answers prayer. When God's people pray earnestly and persistently, it makes a difference. Isaiah prayed that Jerusalem would survive the Assyrian onslaught (37:4), and she did. Hezekiah prayed that his beloved city would be delivered from Sennacherib (37:20), and it happened. When Isaiah said to Hezekiah, "You will not recover" (38:21), Hezekiah prayed for healing (38:2-3), and Isaiah was then able to announce to the court physicians the answer to the king's prayer: "He will recover" (38:22). "The prayer of a righteous man is powerful and effective" (Jas. 5:16).

God takes care of the sin problem. He puts our sins out of sight, behind His back (Isa. 38:17). But He also puts them out of reach—in "the depths of the sea" (Mic. 7:19), removing them from us "as far as the east is from the west" (Ps. 103:12); He puts them out of mind by promising to remember them no more (Jer. 31:34); He puts them out of existence by blotting them out (Ps. 51:1,9; Isa. 43:25), by wiping them out (Acts 3:19), by sweeping them away (Isa. 44:22). Hezekiah knew these glorious truths, and we can too. Because of God's grace, our sins are gone.

For Study or Discussion

1. What is meant by "the Way of Holiness" in Isaiah 35:8? Did anyone before Christ actually walk in it?

2. What events are referred to at the end of chapter 35?

3. What other two places in the Old Testament contain an account of the events in Isaiah 36 and 37? What makes this story worthy of such repetition?

4. What does Hezekiah's poem of 38:10-20 have in common with Psalm 88? What can be concluded from these poems about Old Testament views concerning the afterlife?

5. How does chapter 39 provide a bridge to the exilic setting of the following chapters of Isaiah?

Note
1. "Plague: Clinical Characteristics of the Human Disease," *Encyclopaedia Britannica* (1966), vol. 17, p. 1155.

9

ISAIAH'S CONSOLATION

Isaiah 40—41; 44—45

The Book of Consolation (Isa. 40—66) is the last and longest of the seven basic literary units into which Isaiah's prophecy is divided. Its twenty-seven chapters are further divided into three roughly equal sections of nine chapters apiece. Each section expounds and explains an important doctrinal subject: the doctrine of God, the technical term for which is theology proper (40—48); the doctrine of salvation, technically known as soteriology (49—57); and the doctrine of the last days, technically referred to as eschatology (58—66).

Isaiah himself used "peace," *shālôm* (pronounced shah-LOAM), as a key word to separate the earlier part of his prophecy (1—39) from the latter part (40—66) as well as to divide the latter part into its three distinct nine-chapter sections. "There will be peace and security in my lifetime" is the last sentence in chapter 39. " 'There is no peace,' says the LORD, 'for the wicked'" is the last sentence in chapter 48. "'There is no peace,' says my God, 'for the wicked'" is the last sentence in chapter 57. In addition, the Lord's final poetic message in chapter 66 begins as follows: "I will extend peace to her like a river" (66:12).

The theme of the suffering servant of the Lord is generally agreed to be the most important subject in the latter part of the book of Isaiah. It is introduced to us in chapters 40–48, and its exposition is concluded in chapters 49–57. Because it forms a significant bridge between the theological and soteriological sections of Isaiah's prophecy, we have decided to defer our treatment of the servant theme until after we have completed our study of chapters 40–48 and 49–57. After separating out the main servant passages themselves, we arrive at the following outline for the rest of chapters 40–57: Isaiah's Consolation (40–41; 44–45); Isaiah's Creator (42:5–43:28; 46–48); Isaiah's Redeemer (49:7–50:3; 50:10–52:12; 54–57). We will examine each of these magnificent topics in turn as we proceed through the rest of our commentary.

THE RESTORATION OF JUDAH (Isa. 40:1-11)

It is not difficult to understand why Isaiah 40–66 is called the Book of Consolation. The word "comfort" appears twice (40:1) at the beginning of chapter 40 and three times in a single verse (66:13) in the Lord's final poetic message in chapter 66. In 39:5-7 Isaiah had prophesied that many of Jerusalem's citizens would be taken away into exile to Babylon (605–586 B.C.). Now, in chapters 40–66, he writes as if the Babylonian exile is almost over. In a series of remarkable visions projected into the future to a time 150 years later than his own, Isaiah comforts the people of God by telling them that they will soon be returning to their homeland (beginning in 538 B.C.).

Four voices speak to the despairing exiles in 40:1-11. The first is the voice of grace (40:1-2). God Himself proclaims a message of consolation for His people, using the imperative verb "comfort" twice for emphasis (40:1). Judah's "hard service"—her exile in Babylon—is almost over. She has paid for her sins by enduring the sufferings of captivity. Double comfort is God's gracious response to Judah for the double punishment she has received (40:2).

The second voice is the voice of providence (40:3-5). It is fulfilled ultimately in the voice of John the Baptist (Matt. 3:3; Mark 1:3; Luke 3:4; John 1:23), who would some day insist that repentance is absolutely necessary to prepare the way for Christ to do His saving work (Matt. 3:1-11). But in Isaiah's immediate context the voice of God's messenger commands that a roadbed be prepared and a highway be constructed to enable the Jewish exiles to return from Babylonian captivity. The Lord Himself would lead them, and the procession would be preceded by representatives who would make sure that all obstacles had been cleared out of the way (Isa. 40:3-4). When God redeemed Judah from Babylon, all the nations would witness that glorious event (40:5; 52:10).

The third voice is the voice of assurance (40:6-8). The Lord continues to comfort His people by reminding them that the power of the Babylonians is temporary at best (40:6). As soon as God blows on them, they will wither and vanish (40:7). Peter's quotation of the message of the third voice (1 Pet. 1:24-25) draws from it the enduring principle that the word of the Lord stands forever and is therefore available to us today.

The fourth voice is the voice of hope (40:9-11). The announcement that God is about to lead His people back to Jerusalem is good news indeed (40:9). The proclamation that God is coming, that He is already here (40:9), is one of the central themes of Holy Scripture. It applies to the restoration of Judah from Babylonian exile (52:7-9), to the triumphal entry of the Messiah into Jerusalem (Zech. 9:9; Matt. 21:5), and ultimately to the second coming of Christ (Isa. 62:11; Rev. 22:12). Isaiah foresaw that the Lord's arm, at one and the same time both strong and gentle, would destroy the Babylonians with mighty power and bring back the Jewish exiles with tender compassion (Isa. 40:10-11).

THE OMNIPOTENCE OF GOD (Isa. 40:12-31)

The Lord's sovereignty and power dominate the rest of chapter 40. The series of questions asked by God and His prophet remind us of the long list of difficult questions directed to Job by the Lord in Job 38–41. Like Job, God's people in exile needed to learn that the Lord is worthy of praise because His majesty and power (Isa. 40:12-26) guarantee His goodness and mercy (40:27-31).

To an infinite and all-powerful God, everything else seems small and puny by comparison. All the waters on earth can fit in His hand (40:12), all the nations are like a "drop in a bucket" (40:15) to Him, all the cedar trees of Lebanon cannot suffice to fuel enough fires for consuming the animal sacrifices worthy of His greatness (40:16), all the people on earth are like grasshoppers in His sight (40:22), all the stars in heaven are known intimately by Him (40:26). No one can completely understand Him or instruct Him or teach Him (40:13-14). Nations (40:17), rulers (40:23-24), idols (40:19-20)—He regards them as worthless and brings them to naught. No one, whether in heaven or on earth, is His equal; none can be compared to Him (40:18,25). His surpassing greatness has been obvious to all from the beginning, so no one is without excuse (40:21,28).

Paul quotes 40:13 in Romans 11:34 and also in 1 Corinthians 2:16. The first citation is part of a doxology that praises the Lord for His wisdom and knowledge, both of which in the final analysis are beyond human understanding. In the context of the second citation Paul insists that since no one can perfectly understand the mind of God, therefore only to the extent that "we have the mind of Christ" are we able to recognize God's truth and be delivered from spiritual bondage to other teachers.

It is this kind of all-wise and all-knowing God who is qualified to rescue and restore captive Judah—but only if they trust Him, place their faith in Him, draw their strength from Him, and wait for Him to act (Isa. 40:27-31). The Lord's people in exile complained only because they became impatient and felt that God had ignored them (40:27). But He is the God of infinite resources—and just as He never grows tired or weary (40:28), so also His people need not grow tired or weary because He promises to renew their strength if they place their hope in Him (40:31). The Hebrew verb translated "renew" in 40:31 means literally "exchange." The Lord exchanges our weakness for His strength, so that His power can be made perfect in our weakness (2 Cor. 12:9).

THE PROVIDENCE OF GOD (Isa. 41)

Just as chapter 40 closes with the promise that God's faithful people will "renew their strength" (40:31), so also chapter 41 opens with the Lord's challenge to the nations to "renew their strength" (41:1). All attempts to do so would be futile, while failure to do so would prove fatal. The nations—including Babylon—are on the horns of a dilemma, and there is no escape.

Why so? Because the great Babylonian empire is about to be replaced by the even greater Persian empire. The Lord has "stirred up" Cyrus the Great, king of Persia (559–530 B.C.), from his eastern homeland (41:2). Early in his reign Cyrus conquered kingdoms to the north (41:25), and by 546 B.C., he had reached the west coast of Asia Minor. There he subdued kings (41:2) of the stature of Croesus, the ruler of Lydia. It is no wonder that the nations trembled at Cyrus's approach, that they entered into alliances with one another, that they increased the production of idols in a series of desperate attempts to appease their gods and gain their favor (41:5-7).

But there was one nation that had no need to fear (41:10): "Little Israel" (41:14)! Although the people of Judah were in exile in Babylon, they were still God's people, and He was with them (41:10). He had chosen them to be His own (41:8-9). He had promised that He would help them (41:10,13-14). He had assured them that He would take care of their needs, whether material (41:17-20) or military (41:15-16). He had pledged Himself to be their Redeemer (41:14), the one who would bring them back to their homeland, who would deliver them from their captors, who would free them from shame and disgrace, who would guarantee their present freedom and their future descendants. And all of these things he predicted—long before they happened—through the prophet Isaiah, whom he gave to Jerusalem as a "messenger of good tidings" (41:27).

Judah in exile needed to be reminded often of God's providence to them in former times. The Lord had been especially close to their ancestor Abraham—so much so that Abraham could be rightly called God's "friend" (41:8; 2 Chron. 20:7; Jas. 2:23).

The Lord had often supplied them with water when they were thirsty (Exod. 15:22-27; 17:1-7), and He would do so again (Isa. 41:17-18). He had provided them with acacia wood to build their Tabernacle (Exod. 26:15-28) and with cedarwood to adorn their Temple (1 Kings 5:5-6), and He would supply them again with these trees and others to beautify the desert (Isa. 41:19) and the new Temple that they would build (60:13; Ezra 3:7).

All of this would happen so that everyone would know that the one true God, not the many false gods, had done it (Isa. 41:20). The idols of the pagan nations were unable to adequately explain things that had happened in the past (41:22), much less to accurately predict the future (41:23,26). They, their deeds and their worshipers amounted to nothing (41:24,29), then as now. Judah in exile would learn that important truth, and they would remember it for all time to come.

THE ELECTION OF ISRAEL (Isa. 44:1-5)

Isaiah 41:8-9 introduces us to the servant theme in the book of Isaiah, and 44:1-5 (among many other passages) continues to expound it. Though sometimes the servant is clearly an individual, here he is just as clearly the nation of Israel (44:1-2; see also 41:8-9). God's people are here called "Jeshurun" (meaning "upright"), a term used of them elsewhere only in Deuteronomy 32:15; 33:5,26. But Israel was declared to be upright not because of their inherent goodness but because of God's grace. God elected them, God chose them (Isa. 41:8-9; 44:1-2), to belong to Him (44:5), to be "His people, his treasured possession" (Deut. 7:6). In obedient submission to the Lord, Israel was to be His servant. And some day, when the Messiah came, God would pour out His Spirit on His people (Isa. 44:3; Joel 2:28).

THE IMPOTENCE OF IDOLS (Isa. 44:6-23)

In the meantime, however, the people of Judah would continue to be enticed by idolatry, despite the obvious folly of worshiping statues made of metal or wood or stone. As we have seen already, the prophet Isaiah was unsparing in his sarcasm as he ridiculed idols and idolatry—and nowhere more powerfully than in 44:6-23.

This remarkable section of Scripture begins with the Lord's declaration that apart from Him there is no God (44:6,8). In fact, He challenges anyone to dispute it (44:7). No one accepts the challenge, of course—because God Himself is the only Rock, the only King, the only Redeemer.

The prophet Isaiah is the speaker in 44:9-20. He affirms that idols are worthless (44:9) and that idolmakers are blind, ignorant, and doomed to destruction. In short, all who make and worship idols are nothing (44:9-11).

After dismissing metal idols in a single verse (44:12), Isaiah reserves his most biting scorn for wooden idols (44:13-20), which were the only kind that the average person could afford to purchase (40:20). Though the idolmaker may grow faint (44:12), God never does (40:28). Though man was made in the image of God (Gen. 1:26-27), an idol is shaped "in the form of man" (Isa. 44:13; Deut. 4:16; Rom. 1:23). Though an idol lives in a shrine (Isa. 44:13), the one true God "does not live in temples built by hands" (Acts 17:24). And now comes the supreme irony: The idolmaker cuts down a tree, uses half its wood to build a fire for cooking and for warmth, fashions an idol from the other half—and thinks his actions are completely rational (Isa. 44:14-

20). In actual fact, of course, they are detestable, as are the idols themselves (44:19; 1 Kings 11:5,7; 2 Kings 23:13) as well as those who worship them (Isa. 41:24).

An idol is powerless; it is a mere "block of wood" (44:19). But not so the Lord, who creates (44:21) and redeems (44:22) and displays His glory (44:23). In thoughtful humility, His people repent (44:22); in joyful response, all nature sings (44:23).

THE MISSION OF CYRUS (Isa. 44:24—45:25)

Although Cyrus the Great, founder of the Persian empire, was referred to in a preliminary way in 41:2 and 41:25, he is now specifically mentioned by name (44:28; 45:1). He conquered the city of Babylon in 539 B.C., and the following year he permitted the Jewish exiles there to return to their homeland (45:13). In connection with that memorable event Cyrus issued a decree that authorized the rebuilding of the Temple in Jerusalem (44:28; Ezra 1:2-4; 6:3-5), which in turn would lead to the restoration of the city itself under Nehemiah.

Cyrus was a pagan who did not acknowledge the Lord as the one true God (Isa. 45:4-5). His own inscriptions offer praise to Marduk, who was the chief god of Babylon (Jer. 50:2). But those same inscriptions portray Cyrus as an enlightened and benevolent ruler who was genuinely concerned about the well-being of his own subjects as well as of conquered peoples. Tolerant of all religions, he provided funds to assist the Jews in the reconstruction of their house of worship.

It is obvious that King Cyrus was the human instrument used by the Lord of the universe to set His people free. In fact, the sovereignty of God is the underlying theme of Isaiah 44:24—45:25. The apostle

Paul, in the midst of the greatest of his discussions of divine sovereignty, quotes from 45:9 in Romans 9:20. After all, the Lord is the Redeemer who has created all things (Isa. 44:24; 45:7-8,12,18), who overthrows human wisdom (44:25) and unmasks the folly of idols and their worshipers (45:16,20), who fulfills the predictions of His prophets (44:26; 45:11,19,21), who controls the forces of nature (44:27) and determines the destinies of His creatures (45:9-10,14,17,24-25).

And although Cyrus the Great may have been unaware of it, God determined his destiny as well. Whether he liked it or not, Cyrus would accomplish everything the Lord wanted him to (44:28). God said of Cyrus, "He is my shepherd"—that is, the Lord's prince or ruler (2 Sam. 5:2; Jer. 23:2; Ezek. 34:23-24). So important was Cyrus in God's plans that he is the only pagan in the Old Testament ever to be called the Lord's "anointed" (Isa. 45:1), a "title of honor" (45:4), a term otherwise reserved for the leaders of God's chosen people. Unlike the rulers of Babylon, who had traditionally seized the hand of a statue of Marduk in a futile attempt to gain his blessing, Cyrus would be favored by the Lord Himself, who would graciously take hold of his right hand and make him invincible (45:1). God would call Cyrus by name (45:3-4), which is an Old Testament way of saying that the Lord would choose him and empower him to do his will. Cyrus, the pagan Persian, would free the people of God at his command. Although Palestine was now empty (like the earth at the time of its creation—Gen. 1:2), it would soon be inhabited again (Isa. 45:18; 44:26), and Cyrus would be the instrument used by God to fulfill His holy purpose for His people.

THEMES FROM ISAIAH 40—41; 44—45

Several characteristics and attributes of God stand out in these chapters:

He is the God of comfort. He consoles His exiled people and tells them that their captivity is almost over (40:1-2). He tenderly carries them in His arms and leads them back to the land of Judah (40:11). He tells them not to be afraid because He will strengthen and help them (41:10,13). He is "the Father of compassion and the God of all comfort, who comforts us in all our troubles" (2 Cor. 1:3-4).

He is eternal. The Lord is the everlasting God (Isa. 40:28) who has existed from the beginning (41:4). He is the first and the last (44:6), the Alpha and the Omega, the "Beginning and the End" (Rev. 22:13). From everlasting to everlasting, He is God (Psa. 90:2).

He is omniscient. Our God knows all things. The past, present and future are an open book to Him (41:22-23,26-27). He foreknows everything, and He determines and announces future events (42:9).

He is omnipotent. The Lord is supreme in power and sovereign in purpose. He creates and preserves all things (40:12-17,22-26,28; 44:24; 45:7,12,18). He is sovereign in the affairs of nations (40:22-23), groups of people (40:29-31), and individuals (44:24-28; 45:1-6). His plans for Judah are sure of fulfillment (41:8-10; 42:6-7; 45:13,25).

He is righteous. God displayed His righteousness in His choice of Cyrus as the human agent to set the Jewish exiles free (41:2; 45:13). The release of the captive people of Judah was itself an example of His righteous nature (41:10). His ways are righteous, and His words declare what is right (45:19). And His righteousness (45:24) makes possible the righteousness of His people (45:25).

Righteous in His speech, the Lord swears by Himself (45:23) because He can swear by no one greater (Heb. 6:13). What He utters has eternal significance for all mankind: "Before me every knee will bow; by me every tongue will swear" (Isa. 45:23). Paul considered this verse so important that he quoted from it twice (Rom. 14:11; Phil. 2:10-11) in reference to the exaltation of Jesus Christ as supreme over all.

The righteousness of God shines forth most preeminently in His gracious gift of salvation. In the middle of the nineteenth century, Charles Haddon Spurgeon, not yet sixteen years old, was converted to faith in Christ after hearing a layman's sermon on Isaiah 45:22: "Turn to me and be saved, all you ends of the earth; for I am God, and there is no other."

God, who alone is righteous, alone can save.

For Study or Discussion

1. How far was Isaiah looking into the future when he wrote the chapters beginning at 40?

2. Where does the New Testament connect Jesus directly with Isaiah 40:3?

3. Verses 22-24 of chapter 41 show how corrupting is the choice of a lie for one's ultimate allegiance. Give modern examples of this principle.

4. Verse 6 of chapter 44 refers to God as "the first and . . . the last." Who else in the Bible is referred to in this way, and where?

5. Discuss the implications of 45:7, referring also to Job 2:10, Amos 3:6 and Romans 11:36.

6. Where is 45:23 quoted in the New Testament, and in reference to whom?

10

ISAIAH'S CREATOR

Isaiah 42:5—43:28; 46—48

As we continue our study of theology proper in Isaiah 40—48, we will now emphasize the prophet's understanding of God as the Creator of all that exists. Isaiah 42:5—43:28 and chapters 46—48 are especially well suited for this purpose. The first of the two sections has to do with God's relationship to Israel, while chapters 46—48 are concerned with His judgment on Babylon.

GOD AND ISRAEL (Isa. 42:5—43:28)

God Alone Is Worthy of Praise (42:5-17)

The Lord's sovereign power over His creation, both of the universe and of mankind (42:5), gives substance to His message to the people of Judah. As He summoned Cyrus the Great in righteousness (41:2), so also He calls the servant (42:1,6); as He took hold of the hand of Cyrus (45:1), so also He will take hold of the servant's hand (42:6). Jesus Himself is the supreme fulfillment of the servant prophecy here, as the quotation of 42:1-4 in Matthew 12:15-21 assures us. But the language of Isaiah 42:6-7 is capable of broader application as well, since Jesus used it of the apostle Paul in Acts 26:15-18. The servant would be a "light for the Gentiles" (Isa. 42:6; 49:6), a role filled by Jesus as the "Savior of the world" (1 John 4:14) and by Paul as the "apostle to the Gentiles" (Rom. 11:13).

God is the only one who can declare what will take place in the future, including such "new things" (Isa. 42:9) as the restoration of the Jews from exile in Babylon. He refuses to share His glory with idols (42:8), and their worshipers will be thoroughly disgraced (42:17). The Lord alone is worthy of praise, and Isaiah calls on the whole earth to sing a new song to Him (42:10-13).

The Lord responds by declaring His intention to free His captive people. He has kept silent for a "long time" (42:14)—almost seventy years (Jer. 25:11-12; 29:10)—but now He will remove the obstacles, both physical and spiritual, that might otherwise prevent the Jews from making the effort to return to their homeland (Isa. 42:15-16). Although at one time He restrained Himself (42:14) so that His people might be punished through exile (40:2), He would no longer forsake them (42:16).

Israel is Blind and Sinful (42:18-25)

Unlike the servant earlier in chapter 42, the servant here (42:19) is the people of Israel (as in 41:8-9). Spiritually speaking, they are deaf and blind (42:18). Although they should be serving God faithfully, they refuse to see His mighty acts on their behalf or hear His words of comfort and encouragement (42:20; 6:9-10). The Lord had graciously given them His law (42:21) on Mount Sinai (Exod. 24:3; 34:29-32), but they sinned against Him and refused to obey Him (Isa. 42:24).

God therefore handed His people over to be "plundered and looted" (42:22), first by the Assyrians (10:5-6) and then by the Babylonians (39:6). Jerusalem was destroyed by Nebuchadnezzar of Babylon in 586 B.C., and the Temple built by Solomon was burned to the ground (2 Kings 25:9). But in spite of the fact that the Lord's hand of judgment was heavy on His people, by and large they did not repent (Isa. 42:25).

God Is Merciful and Compassionate (Chap. 43)

Just as the Lord had introduced Himself generally as the Creator of heaven and earth in 42:5, so now He introduces Himself specifically as the Creator of Israel (43:1). Although judgment is God's last word for all who persist in their sin (42:25), redemption is His message to sinners who repent (43:1). He is indeed a "gracious and compassionate God, slow to anger and abounding in love" (Jon. 4:2). In choosing Cyrus the Great, the Lord had called him by name (Isa. 45:3-4). He would now do the same for Israel, and they would become His (43:1).

In former days He had brought Israel's ancestors through the waters of the Red Sea (43:16; Exod. 14:21-22) and the Jordan River (Josh. 3:14-17), and He was prepared to perform similar miracles for His people again if necessary (Isa. 43:2). Likewise the danger of fire poses no threat to those who belong to the Lord (43:2), as He would some day prove in the experience of Shadrach, Meshach, and Abednego (Dan. 3:25-27). The redemption of the Jews from Babylonian exile was to be illustrated when the Persians conquered Egypt, Cush, and Seba, because those three nations would be given as a ransom to Persia in exchange for her kindness to captive Judah (Isa. 43:3-4). The Jews would be liberated not only from Babylon in the east but also from the islands and coastlands of the west (43:5; 11:11), from Hamath in the north (43:6; 10:9), and from Egypt in the south (43:6). The Lord had created and formed His people, and they were His (43:7).

Isaiah 43:9-13 portrays a court scene in which the nations are called on to bring their own witnesses to testify on their behalf (43:9), but to no avail. The people of Israel are the Lord's only true witnesses, and God's work on their behalf is undeniable proof of His saving power (43:10). No foreign god can do what the Lord does: He reveals the future, He saves from past bondage, and He proclaims His power in the present (43:12). When He determines a particular course of action, no one can stop Him (43:13)—not even the mighty Babylonians, who would soon become fugitives in their own ships (43:14).

The Lord reminds His people that this is not the time for them to remember how He brought them through the Red Sea (43:16) and destroyed the Pharaoh's chariots (43:17; Exod. 14:28; 15:4). The Jews were not to dwell on the past, because the Lord was going to perform new miracles for them (Isa. 43:18): He would build a highway through the desert and provide water for His people to drink (43:19-20) as they left Babylon and headed westward for Jerusalem.

But the Lord reminds His people also that although in the past they had brought sacrifices in abundance to Him (1:11-15), they had done so from improper motivation and sinful hearts (43:24). No amount of sacrifice is acceptable to God under such circumstances, and it is just as though they had brought nothing to Him at all. The Lord's demands were by no means excessive (43:23), but His people prayed halfheartedly and served Him listlessly

(43:22). None of them was innocent (43:26), since even Abraham and their other spiritual leaders were sinners (43:27; Gen. 12:18; 20:9; Isa. 9:15; 28:7).

Land and Temple would therefore be destroyed (43:28). But despite the terrible punishment Israel would receive, God would remain eager to forgive His people if they were willing to repent. He would wipe out their sins (Acts 3:19), He would blot out their transgressions (Isa. 43:25), He would sweep away their offenses (44:22)—not for their sakes, but for His own glory (43:25).

GOD AND BABYLON (Isa. 46—48)

Babylon's Gods Are Doomed (Chap. 46)

Isaiah, worshiper of the one true God, who is the Creator of heaven and earth, knew that all so-called gods are impotent and meaningless. He therefore envisioned the gods of Babylon in humiliation and disgrace (46:1), themselves carried off into exile (46:2) at the time of Babylon's capture by Cyrus in 539 B.C. *Bel* (46:1) was the Babylonian word for "lord" and was another name for Marduk (Jer. 50:2), the chief deity of Babylon. Nebo was believed to be the son of Marduk and was the Babylonian god of learning and writing. But both deities were merely figments of the imagination, and their images were products of the goldsmith's craft (Isa. 46:6). Unlike the God of Israel, who carried His people in His arms (46:3-4), the gods of Babylon were themselves carried on the shoulders of their worshipers (46:7). Unable to move and powerless to speak, Marduk and Nebo could neither hear nor save their followers (46:7).

The Lord, however, can both hear and save (46:4). None can compare with Him (46:5), because He is the only God who matters (46:9). His purpose for the remnant of His people (46:3) would soon be fulfilled (46:10) in the coming of Cyrus, who is pictured as a bird of prey "from a far-off land" (46:11). He would serve as the Lord's anointed (45:1) to bring release from the political oppression of Babylon (46:13) and slavery to the worshipers of Babylon's helpless gods (46:2).

Babylon's Empire Will Fall (Chap. 47)

Apart from 47:4, which is an exclamation of praise by Isaiah himself, the rest of chapter 47 is the words of the Lord to the city of Babylon, announcing to her that her powerful empire will soon be no more.

The resurgence of Babylonian might had begun in 626 B.C. under an able ruler named Nabopolassar. His son Nebuchadnezzar II came to the throne in 605 and reigned until 562, beautifying the city and strengthening the empire during his long period of rule. He built the famous hanging gardens of Babylon, one of the seven wonders of the ancient world, to relieve the homesickness of his Median queen for the verdant mountains of her native land. The beautiful Babylon of Nebuchadnezzar could justly be called "queen of kingdoms" (47:5).

But Nebuchadnezzar was followed by a succession of weak rulers, and by 539 B.C. Babylon's doom was sealed. Although since 626 she had been a virgin (47:1) in the sense that her walls had never been breached and she had never been conquered, her nakedness would soon be exposed (47:3) and she would be a virgin no longer. Though formerly happy and carefree (21:5), her people would soon sit in the dust and mourn (47:1). Once wealthy beyond belief, they would soon be reduced to the menial task of grinding flour by hand (47:2; Exod. 11:5). Though they had deported many captive peoples, they themselves would soon "wade through the streams" (Isa. 47:2) into the darkness of exile (47:5).

Beginning in 605 B.C., the Lord had used captivity as a means of punishing the people of Judah for their sins, and Babylon had been His instrument of judgment. But the Babylonians had been ruthless and merciless, showing no compassion even to the elderly (47:6). In addition the Babylonian rulers made pretensions to deity, considering themselves to be virtually gods (14:13-14). Similarly the city of Babylon herself said, "I am, and there is none besides me" (47:8,10). And to her claims of uniqueness she added claims of eternity: "I will continue forever" (47:7). She tried to give substance to such fantasies with the help of astrologers and stargazers (47:13) and by using sorceries and magic spells (47:10,12).

But all would be in vain, and her pride (47:8) would be her undoing. Like a widow she would soon be deserted and in distress, and her people would be deported or killed (47:9). Disaster, calamity and catastrophe would be her fate (47:11), and they would overtake her without warning, "on a single day" (47:9)—October 13, 539 B.C.—when the armies of Cyrus the Great would seize Babylon and slay King Belshazzar (Dan. 5:30-31), whose name ironically means "Bel (Marduk), protect the king!"

Nothing Babylon could do would ward off her final destruction. Demanding unconditional surrender, the Medes and Persians would not accept a ransom (Isa. 47:11). Babylon's finest counselors, unable even to save themselves, would be burned up like stubble in a conflagration (47:14-15). The fire that would consume them would have "no coals to warm anyone" (47:14)—a subtle reference to the use of firewood, a material from which pagans sometimes made idols (44:15,19). And once again the Holy One of Israel

(47:4) would prove to be infinitely mightier than the unholy gods of Babylon.

Babylon's Captives Will Be Released (Chap. 48)

Isaiah 48 is divided into two equal halves of eleven verses apiece, and each half begins with the Lord's command to His people: "Listen" (48:1,12). The first half reminds the people of Judah of their privileged position as members of the house of Jacob (48:1) and as citizens of Jerusalem (48:2). Although they "rely on the God of Israel" (48:2), they do not always do so sincerely (48:1). They are often stubborn (48:4) and disobedient (48:8), even though the Lord has worked on their behalf time and time again (48:3,6). And now they find themselves in exile, in the "furnace of affliction" (48:10). The destruction of Jerusalem by the Babylonians had brought dishonor to the name of the Lord (48:11; Ezek. 20:9,14,22; 36:20-23). Jerusalem's people deserved further judgment, but the Lord would delay His wrath for His own name's sake and would not totally annihilate them (Isa. 48:9). Despite their continued unfaithfulness, he would free them from their Babylonian captors. His intention to deliver His people is the subject of the second half of Isaiah 48.

Gracious and loving to the very end, the Lord continues to deal with His wayward followers. If they had not been so incurably rebellious, the Abrahamic promise of numberless descendants (Gen. 13:16; 22:17) would have been fulfilled in their own generation (Isa. 48:19) as it had been in the days of King Solomon (1 Kings 4:20). They would have had peace in abundance (Isa. 48:18), but there is no peace for the wicked (48:22). Nevertheless the Lord, Creator of heaven and earth (48:13), He who had called His people (48:12), would now redeem them. He who had miraculously provided their ancestors with water in the Sinai desert after the Exodus (48:21; Exod. 17:6; Num. 20:11) would now supply His people with water in the eastern deserts after the exile. His "chosen ally" (Isa. 48:14), Cyrus the Great, would carry out God's purpose against Babylon and would succeed in his mission (48:15).

And so the prophet Isaiah, conscious of the Lord's presence and call (48:16), peers into the distant future and commands the exiles: "Leave Babylon, flee from the Babylonians!" (48:20). He says this not because the Jews would be compelled to flee (52:12) but because terrible judgment was soon to fall on Babylon.

After Isaiah 48:20, the prophet never again mentions Babylon or the Babylonians by name.

THEMES FROM ISAIAH 42:5—43:28; 46—48

The Lord is the only God. No god was formed before Him, and no god will exist after Him (43:10). Apart from Him there is no one who can save (43:11; 47:13-15). He is the only one who has the ability to predict the future (42:9; 43:9,19; 46:10; 48:3,5-7). Because of His mighty acts in the past He is the only one who can say, "I am God, and there is none like me" (46:9).

Who else but the Lord of the universe could possibly say, "I am God, and there is no other" (46:9)? The city of Babylon arrogantly said something similar of herself (47:8,10), but the Lord rebuked her and then destroyed her. Foreign gods cannot reveal or save or proclaim (43:12); only the one true God can perform such gracious acts. The Lord tenderly carries His people (46:3-4), while idols need to be carried themselves (46:1,7). The Lord answers when His people call (58:9), but idols are unable to answer (46:7).

The Lord is a God of grace. Although His people
do not deserve to be forgiven, He blots out their transgressions and remembers their sins no more—not
primarily for their sakes, but for His own sake
(43:25). He delays His wrath against them—not primarily for their sakes, but for His own name's sake
(48:9). He holds back His punishment from them—
not primarily for their sakes, but for the sake of His
praise (48:9), since He alone is worthy of praise. He
tests His people in the furnace of affliction (48:10)
and says of Himself that it is "for my own sake, for my
own sake" (48:11).

Grace is undeserved merit, unearned affection,
aggressive love. The Lord's common grace, His
redemptive grace, His ultimate grace in eternity—all
come to us not because of what we are but because of
who He is. The Lord is the "God of all grace" (1 Pet.
5:10).

The Lord is a God of compassion. He is not only
concerned about His people from the moment of their
birth (Isa. 46:3); He also sustains them to the end of
their lives (46:4). Though His people are "far from
righteousness" (46:12), in His compassion He brings
His own righteousness near and grants salvation to
Israel (46:13). Though His people often pay no attention to His commands (48:18), in compassion He
redeems them (48:20).

But because the Lord is merciful, He expects all
who are created in His image to be compassionate as
well. Even when they are the instruments of His judgment, if they show no mercy He punishes them (47:5-
9).

The Lord is a God of judgment. This facet of the
Lord's character is closely related to the point just
made: The instruments of God's judgment are themselves not exempt from God's judgment. Israel would

be judged by Babylon (47:6), and Babylon would in turn be judged by Persia (48:14). When people (whether they are God's chosen people or not) worship idols, they can expect to face divine punishment (46:1-2). When they are cruel and ruthless, God's wrath is not far away (47:6-7). When they sin openly and persistently, the judgment they least expect will overtake them in full measure (47:8-9). When they are wicked and arrogant, inescapable disaster will fall upon them (47:10-11). When they engage in demonic and occult practices, they will not be able to save themselves from the flames of divine judgment (47:12-15).

Isaiah 40—48, the most important section of the Old Testament on the subject of theology proper (the doctrine of God), begins with this exhilarating statement: "Comfort, comfort my people, says your God" (40:1). It ends, however, with this sobering statement: " 'There is no peace,' says the LORD, 'for the wicked'" (48:22). Although it is not God's will that anyone should perish, life eternal in His presence is contingent on repentance (2 Pet. 3:9). If it be true that man's sin (Gen. 6:5) is God's sorrow (Gen. 6:6), it is equally true that man's sin (Gen. 6:12) brings God's judgment (Gen. 6:13).

To use the words of Isaiah: "They would not follow his ways; they did not obey his law. So he poured out on them his burning anger" (Isa. 42:24-25).

For Study or Discussion

1. Which verses in these chapters help to deliver the message that "the Lord is the only God"? How would these claims sound if they originated in the twentieth century?

2. What do Isaiah 43:25; 48:9 and 48:11 have to say about the grace of God?

3. What was motivating God's compassion in these chapters? How does His compassion toward the Church differ from this?

4. What kind of balance is reached in Isaiah between God's compassion and God's judgment? What effect does the New Testament have over that balance?

5. What happens when either of these facets of God's character is overemphasized?

11

ISAIAH'S REDEEMER

Isaiah 49:7–50:3; 50:10–52:12; 54–57

The second and central section of the Book of Consolation (Isa. 40–66) is, like each of the other two sections, nine chapters in length. Consisting of chapters 49–57, it deals with the subject of soteriology (the doctrine of salvation) and therefore emphasizes God as Saviour and Redeemer. It also contains the last three of the four servant songs found in the Book of Consolation, and in so doing it highlights the redemptive ministry of the suffering servant of the Lord. After separating out the three servant passages for later treatment along with the first of them, we are left with a series of sections that are concerned mostly (though not exclusively) with God's relationship to the city of Jerusalem. A key verse in these chapters is 52:1: "Awake, awake, O Zion, clothe yourself with strength. Put on your garments of splendor, O Jerusalem, the holy city."

THE CONSOLATION OF ZION (Isa. 49:7–50:3)

The Lord is introduced to us immediately as Israel's Redeemer (49:7). He speaks to the suffering servant, the one who was despised (49:7; 53:3), and tells

Him that kings will bow down before Him (49:7; 52:15). Zion, also despised, will be similarly honored by her former oppressors (60:14) because of God's faithfulness to His people. Just as in the Year of Jubilee enslaved debtors were to be freed and allowed to return to their family property (Lev. 25:10,13,54), so also the return from Babylonian exile would free the captive Jews and restore their homeland and city to them (Isa. 49:8-9). In 2 Corinthians 6:2, Paul quotes the first two lines of Isaiah 49:8 to illustrate the far greater deliverance brought about through the redemptive work of Christ. The phrase "day of salvation" takes on a new and fuller meaning because of what Jesus has done for us.

The Lord will have compassion on His newly-released people as they return from Babylon to Judah and Jerusalem. He will give them food and water and protection from the desert sun (49:9-10). Well-built roads will make their travel easy (49:11). They will come from all directions—not only from Babylon in the east, but also from the north and from the west and from the region of Sinim (49:12), a reference to the inhabitants of Aswan in the southern part of Egypt (Ezek. 29:10; 30:6). Pictures of heaven are not frequent in Scripture, but in Revelation 7:16-17 John paints one for us that makes generous use of the phraseology of Isaiah 49:10.

The prophet calls on heaven and earth to rejoice because of the Lord's care and concern for His people (49:13), but Zion—not yet restored—feels forsaken and forgotten (49:14). So the Lord responds with four illustrations to underscore the fact that He will never forget His people: (1) Though a mother may forget her nursing infant, God will never forget Zion (49:15); (2) the Lord has a sketch of Jerusalem tattooed on the palms of His hands, making it impos-

sible for Him to forget her (49:16); (3) wherever He
turns, He sees the walls of Zion standing before Him
(49:16); and (4) the Lord can no more forget the
returning exiles who will inhabit Jerusalem than a
bride can forget the ornaments she wears (49:18).
Zion, now desolate and barren, will be astonished to
see the large numbers of people returning to live
there again (49:21). In fact, she will be too small to
hold them all (49:19-20; Zech. 2:4; 10:10).

Continuing to comfort Zion, the Lord tells her
that Gentiles (such as the Persians) will assist the
Jews in their return from exile (Isa. 49:22) and that
kings (such as Cyrus the Great) will provide for their
needs and, in so doing, demonstrate that God is sovereign (49:23). The prophet asks rhetorically whether
anyone is mighty enough to compel the Babylonians
to give up their plunder and release their captives
(49:24). The Lord then responds by saying that He
Himself will force the issue and that the restoration
of Judah will go on as planned (49:25). In addition,
just as Jerusalem's people were reduced to cannibal-
ism during the final days of their siege in 586 B.C.
(Lam. 4:10), so also Zion's oppressors would find it
necessary to "eat their own flesh" (Isa. 49:26).

Why did Judah go into exile in the first place?
Because of her sins (50:1). The Lord was ready to
help His people, but they refused to repent. Before
the Exodus from Egypt He made the fish in the Nile
rot as a result of the first plague (Exod. 7:21), sent
darkness over the land in the ninth plague (10:21-
22), and enabled the Israelites to go through the Red
Sea on dry ground (14:21-22). A God who could perform such miracles in preparation for an exodus
could surely do whatever was necessary to bring His
people back from exile (Isa. 50:2-3). But Judah had
broken her relationship with God by sinning against

Him, by initiating divorce proceedings against Him, by leaving Him no option but to send her away with a certificate of divorce and sell her to His creditors (50:1). Nevertheless, the Lord could not abandon His people forever. In God's timetable, the exile lasted only a "brief moment" (54:7).

THE ENCOURAGEMENT OF ZION (Isa. 50:10—52:12)

Several striking literary features hold this section of Isaiah's prophecy together. In 51:1,4,7,21, the command "Listen to me" or its equivalent occurs. Repeated imperatives also appear frequently: "Awake, awake" in 51:9,17; 52:1, and "Depart, depart" in 52:11. Such devices lend a note of urgency to the encouraging words the Lord speaks to the people of Jerusalem.

Isaiah begins by contrasting obedient people with those who are disobedient. Though the former may be in the darkness of trouble or distress, they trust in God to help them (50:10). The latter, however, self-righteously light their own torches to illumine the pathway that will lead them out of difficulty—only to receive divine judgment (50:11).

In 51:1-8 the Lord pleads with His chosen people to hear Him out. He asks them to look to their glorious past in order to learn lessons for the future (51:1). Just as God had blessed one man, Abraham (51:2), by making him the ancestor of numberless descendants (Gen. 13:16), so also He would now bless Abraham's offspring who were discouraged and languishing in exile. Just as God had prospered Abraham even though his nephew Lot had selfishly chosen the well-watered plain of the Jordan, which was like Eden, "the garden of the LORD" (Gen. 13:10-11), so also God would now bring the former citizens of Jerusalem out of exile and "make her deserts like Eden, her wastelands like the garden of the LORD" (Isa. 51:3). In the process of rescuing His own people, God would provide justice for the nations as well (51:4-5). Unlike the temporary existence of heaven and earth (Matt. 24:35; 2 Pet. 3:10, Isa. 51:6), God's salvation and righteousness would last forever (51:6,8), supremely because of the redemptive death of Jesus the coming Messiah.

The prophet himself then speaks to the Lord's arm (51:9), symbolic of the divine power that centuries earlier had cut Rahab (a poetic name for Egypt; see 30:7) to pieces and sent the Israelites through the Red Sea dry-shod (51:10). So also now, says Isaiah, the Lord's ransomed people will return to Jerusalem from Babylonian exile (51:11, repeated for emphasis from 35:10). The Lord, Maker of heaven and earth (51:13,16), the all-powerful Creator of the universe (51:15), calms the hearts of His followers (51:12) and assures them that they will "soon be set free" (51:14).

Isaiah next encourages Jerusalem by pointing out to her that although formerly the Lord punished her by making her drink the cup of His wrath (51:17,20), soon that same cup would be mercifully taken out of her hands (51:21-22) and given to her Babylonian tormentors (51:23; 14:4). Like the beautiful garments of Israel's priests, which gave them dignity and honor (Exod. 28:2,40), "garments of splendor" would adorn Zion, and she would again be the "holy city" (Isa. 52:1). The dust of mourning and the chains of captivity would soon be dim memories (52:2), relegated to the past like the Egyptian sojourn and Assyrian oppression (52:4).

In Romans 2:24, Paul makes reference to the language of Isaiah 52:5 and in so doing declares the truth that in every age the name of God is blasphemed by His enemies—sometimes because God's people are themselves rebellious and unfaithful. But, as foretold by Isaiah's God, the day of deliverance from the mocking Babylonians would soon come, and the Lord's ransomed people would honor His name (52:6). Whether through exodus or from exile, God's mighty arm would bring salvation to His people (Exod. 6:6; Isa. 52:10). Jerusalem would burst into song at the encouraging news of her coming redemption (52:9)—a redemption from Babylonian exile that would prefigure Jesus' deliverance from sin, as Paul's quotation of Isaiah 52:7 in Romans 10:15 clearly demonstrates. And just as the return of God and His people to Zion stresses His sovereign rule over the world (Isa. 52:7-8), so also Christ's second coming will usher in His eternal kingdom (1 Cor. 15:24-25; Rev. 11:15; 19:6).

But in the meantime the prophet urges the captives to leave Babylon, telling the priests and Levites who were responsible for carrying the vessels of the Lord (Num. 3:6-8; 2 Chron. 5:5-7) to purify themselves in preparation for the task (Isa. 52:11). Cyrus the Great would allow the exiles to take back to Jerusalem the Temple articles seized by Nebuchadnezzar (Ezra 1:7-11). There would be no need for undue haste, however, because whether through exodus or from exile, God both precedes His people and follows after them, protecting them behind and before (Exod. 13:21; 14:19-20; Isa. 52:12; 58:8).

THE FUTURE GLORY OF ZION (Isa. 54)

In Galatians 4:24-27, the apostle Paul makes figurative application of Isaiah 54:1 to his own situation. In Paul's context the "barren woman" is "the Jerusalem that is above" (Gal. 4:26), a figurative description of Abraham's wife Sarah, producing spiritual offspring, believers in Christ (3:29), "children of promise" (4:28). In Isaiah's context the "barren woman" was Jerusalem during the exile, a city that would need to expand its boundaries (Isa. 54:2) because of the large number of returnees who would soon fill it and spill over into the surrounding areas (54:3).

Judah would be restored, however, not only physically but also spiritually. Shame and disgrace (54:4) would give way to joy and singing (54:1). The slavery that preceded the Exodus in the days of Israel's youth and the temporary period of anguish and suffering (54:7-8) that characterized exile in the days of Jerusalem's widowhood would soon be forgotten (54:4). Jerusalem's Maker was also her Redeemer; Jerusalem's God was also her husband (54:5) who would woo her back to Himself (54:6). The Lord's anger against His people (54:8-9) would be replaced by divine compassion for them (54:7-8,10).

The city of Jerusalem, soon to be rebuilt by the returning exiles, is described in 54:11-12 in figurative terms that are reflected in the picture of the new Jerusalem painted for us in Revelation 21:10,18-21. The first half of Isaiah 54:13 is quoted in John 6:45 to illustrate the principle that God the Father draws people to new understanding of and new life in God the Son. In the restored Jerusalem following the exile, terror and tyranny would be replaced by peace and righteousness (Isa. 54:13-14). God's sovereignty, once directed toward the destruction of His people (54:16), would now be employed only for their benefit (54:17). His chosen ones would be known as "servants of the LORD," spiritual "offspring" of the Lord's suffering servant (53:10).

THE GRACIOUS GOD OF ZION (Isa. 55-57)

A Divine Invitation (Chap. 55)

The background of Isaiah 55 is the Lord's summons to His captive people to return to Jerusalem and be restored physically and spiritually, but the teachings and implications of this great chapter are strikingly contemporary. Spiritual rather than physical thirst is the primary intention of 55:1 (see 44:3). Jesus' offer of "living water" to the Samaritan woman comes immediately to mind (John 4:10,13-14; see also John 7:37-39). God's richest blessings cannot be purchased at any cost (Isa. 55:1). The death of the suffering servant (53:5-9) would some day purchase the free gift of life for all who trust in Him (Rom. 6:23; Rev. 21:6;22:17).

The covenant that God had made with David was everlasting (Isa. 55:3; 2 Sam. 7:14-16), and David's line would some day culminate in the Messiah (Matt. 1:1,17). When Jesus died on the cross, some people doubtless thought that David's dynasty—whether physical or spiritual—had finally come to an end. But then our Lord rose from the dead, and in Jesus' resurrection Paul saw undeniable proof that God's promises to David as recorded in Isaiah 55:3 are indeed eternal (Acts 13:34). David himself had been a "witness to the peoples" (Isa. 55:4) in the sense that he had praised the Lord and exalted Him among the nations (2 Sam. 22:47,50-51), and David's greater son, the Messiah, would also be such a witness, both individually (Isa. 42:6; 49:6) and through His messengers (Acts 13:47). And David was known far and wide as a "leader" (Isa. 55:4; see 1 Sam. 13:14), as was also the Messiah (Dan. 9:25).

Isaiah 55:6-11 stresses the spiritual nature of God's deliverance of His people from exile in Babylon.

They were to seek Him through the window of his availability (55:6), for His timetable would not always make Him accessible to them. Since God's ways and thoughts are higher than ours (55:8-9), sinners must turn to Him only on His terms (55:7). His word and promises are completely dependable, eternally valid (55:11) and impossible to avoid (Heb. 4:12-13).

References to the physical restoration that would accompany the return from exile conclude Isaiah 55. The divine deliverance would be an "everlasting sign" (55:13) that would never be forgotten.

Divine Rewards and Punishments (Chaps. 56–57)

Since the return from exile is "close at hand" (56:1), the Lord warns His people to live righteously and treat one another justly. After the Exodus from Egypt the Sabbath had been established as a sign of the Mosaic covenant (Exod. 31:13-17), and the forth-coming restoration from exile was to be characterized by keeping the Sabbath as a sign of the people's will-ingness to obey God fully (Isa. 56:2,4,6). Neither for-eigners nor eunuchs willing to follow the Lord were to be excluded from worshiping the Lord in the pre-cincts of the new Temple in Jerusalem (55:3-7), although many representatives of both groups had been barred from certain ritual practices in earlier generations (Exod. 12:43; Deut. 23:1,3,7-8). The Ethiopian eunuch who was introduced to Christ by Philip (Acts 8:27,38-40) is a well-known example of the gathering of "still others" besides the "exiles of Israel" (Isa. 56:8). Only by including both Jews and Gentiles could the Lord's Temple truly be called a "house of prayer for all nations" (56:7), a title that may have been anticipated by Solomon in his prayer of dedication for the original Temple (1 Kings 8:41-43). During the lifetime of Solomon's greatest descendant, Jesus Christ, some of the men who were supposed to be serving God in the Jerusalem Temple had begun to turn it into a "den of robbers" (Jer. 7:11; Matt. 21:12-13). The Lord, the "high and lofty One" (Isa. 57:15), is not well served by arrogant and greedy people (57:17,20-21). He is nevertheless patient and forgiving toward those who are repentant (57:15-16,18-19). He therefore welcomes the urgent command that prepares the highway for the long trek of the redeemed exiles from Babylon to Jerusalem (57:14).

But what of the wicked? God's accusations against them occupy the attention of the prophet in 56:9–57:13, and it is not a pretty picture. The foreign invaders of Judah before the exile itself are called "beasts" (56:9), able to ravage a weakened nation because neither prophets (56:10) nor rulers (56:11) are concerned for anything other than their own interests (56:12–57:1). Sorcery, mockery, adultery, idolatry—all were common practices in Judah (57:3-10) before Jerusalem's final fall in 586 B.C. People sometimes sacrificed their children to Molech, the chief god of the Ammonites (1 Kings 11:7), at pagan shrines in the Hinnom Valley (Jer. 32:35) southwest of Jerusalem (Isa. 57:5,9). Divine retribution and judgment are inevitable for all who commit such blatantly vile sins (57:11-13).

A contemporary example that comes to mind is Nazi Germany, which during World War II carried out the mass murder of six million Jews in concentration camps throughout eastern Europe. It is perhaps not merely coincidental that the planners and builders of the main Holocaust monument in modern Jerusalem gave it the name Yad Vashem (pronounced YAHD vah-SHEM), a Hebrew phrase that in Isaiah 56:5—a verse in the immediate context of 56:9–57:13—is translated "a memorial and a name." The monument itself contains records of the Holocaust, a tiled floor displaying the names of the concentration camps, and an eternal flame serving as a perpetual reminder of man's inhumanity to man.

THEMES FROM ISAIAH 49:7–50:3; 50:10–52:12; 54–57

God is always present everywhere. Nothing escapes His notice (49:14-18; 54:7-8; 57:11,18), because He is omnipresent. That He lives in "a high and holy place" emphasizes that He is up there, that He is transcendent; and that He lives also with him who is "contrite and lowly in spirit" (57:15) stresses that He is down here, that He is immanent. We cannot flee from His presence, because He is up and down and east and west all at the same time (Ps. 139:7-10).

God makes covenants with His people. He made a covenant with Noah, stating that floodwaters would never again cover the earth (54:9; Gen. 9:8-17). He made a covenant with Abraham, assuring him that he would be the father of many nations (Isa. 51:2; Gen. 15:4-21;17). He made a covenant with Moses, guaranteeing that Israel would become a kingdom of priests and a holy nation and instituting the Sabbath as the covenant sign (Isa. 56:4,6; Exod. 19:5-6; 24:3-8; 31:12-17). He made a covenant with David, promising him an everlasting dynasty (Isa. 55:3; 2 Sam. 7:11-16). He makes a covenant of peace with all whom He loves (Isa. 54:10)—peace to all, whether far or near (57:19). Such peace characterizes the new covenant in Jesus' blood, a peace preached to those who are near and also to those who are far away (Eph. 2:17). To those who repent of their sins, the Word of God speaks with power: "The promise is for you and

your children and for all who are far off—for all whom
the Lord our God will call" (Acts 2:39).

For Study or Discussion

1. Read Isaiah 51:6, Matthew 24:35 and 2 Peter
   3:10. What are the implications of the temporary
   nature of heaven and earth?

2. Who is the "barren woman" in Isaiah 54, and why
   was she to enlarge the place of her tent?

3. What conclusions can be drawn from Isaiah 54:7
   and 2 Peter 3:8 about God's timetable? How does
   it differ from ours?

4. Discuss the relationship between Isaiah 54:11-12
   and Revelation 21:10-21.

5. How are Isaiah 56:6-7 and Acts 10:9-16 related?

12

ISAIAH'S SERVANT

Isaiah 42:1-4; 49:1-6; 50:4-9;

52:13—53:12

The theme of the suffering servant of the Lord is the most important subject in the book of Isaiah as a whole. Although the servant motif is found throughout the entire book, it is concentrated in the theological (40–48) and soteriological (49–57) sections of the Book of Consolation and most especially in chapters 42–53. Of particular significance are the four basic servant songs, which consist of 42:1-4, 49:1-6, 50:4-9 and 52:13—53:12. Some scholars would extend the limits of the first three songs by adding a few verses to each (for example, 42:1-7 or 42:1-9; 49:1-7 or 49:1-13; 50:4-11), but it is probably best to understand the extra verses as connecting links that serve as transitions from the songs themselves to the passages that follow them.

The phrase "my servant" or its equivalent occurs in 20:3; 22:20; 42:1,19; 43:10; 44:1-2,21; 45:4; 49:3,5-7; 50:10; 52:13; 53:11. The title implies that God has chosen the person or persons so designated and that they are to submit to Him in obedience, worship, and ministry. The identification of the servant is not always uniform. In some cases he is clearly an individual (Eliakim son of Hilkiah in 22:20; Isaiah

himself in 20:3), while in others he is just as clearly a
group of people (for example in 43:10, where "servant" is parallel to "witnesses"). The most frequent
identification is Jacob or Israel (44:1-2,21; 45:4;
49:3), and in such cases only a careful examination
of the context can tell us whether the man named
Jacob, the nation of Israel, or an individual personified as Israel is intended.

In those cases where Isaiah does not tell us who
the servant is (42:1,19; 50:10; 52:13; 53:11), all
sorts of proposals have been made in attempting to
identify him. Individuals suggested have included
Moses, Uzziah, Josiah, Jeremiah, Jehoiachin, Ezekiel, Cyrus, Zerubbabel and, of course, the Messiah.
One of the more clever suggestions has been that the
unnamed servant is Meshullam son of Zerubbabel (1
Chron. 3:19) because in Isaiah 42:19 the phrase "one
committed" is the translation of the Hebrew word
měshullām. But in context the word is much more
likely a common noun than a proper noun, and
almost no one takes seriously the idea that an
obscure son of Zerubbabel was intended as Isaiah's
suffering servant.

Included among the groups of people proposed in
attempts to name the unidentified servant are the
nation of Israel throughout its history, the Israel of
Isaiah's own time, the exiles of 586 B.C., the spiritual
remnant within Israel, and ideal Israel as opposed to
the actual Israel of experience. One of the more inter-
esting proposals, which tries to combine the identification of the servant as an individual with his identification as a corporate or group entity, is that the
servant was David's dynasty as personified in one of
its kings (Jehoiachin or Zedekiah, for example).

What shall we say to all of the above? Is it possible
to identify the servant in those verses where Isaiah

himself does not do so? For that matter, how can we tell whether the servant "Israel" is the nation or a personified individual? And here is an even more tantalizing idea: Could it be that the unnamed servant is a group and an individual at one and the same time—or at least that he is sometimes a group, sometimes an individual?

Perhaps the best way of understanding Isaiah's servant is to observe that there seems to be a gradual development in the prophet's own conception of who the servant was and what he did. It is helpful to diagram the process in terms of a pyramid or of a cone resting on its circular face. At the base of the pyramid or cone is the entire nation of Israel, chosen by God to serve Him (41:8-10; 42:18-19). Halfway up the pyramid or cone is the faithful remnant, the spiritually sensitive people within the larger nation (43:1-2; 44:1-2,21-22). And at the apex is the suffering individual, the servant Messiah, He who would be obedient even to the point of death itself (52:13—53:12). Needless to say, this progression in Isaiah's understanding leaves room for the possibility that in some of the other earlier passages we should interpret the servant as an individual by way of anticipation. In fact, in all four of the basic servant songs the messianic interpretation is the best way to handle the data, as we shall see.

THE SERVANT'S CALL (Isa. 42:1-4)

Just as the servant is God's "chosen one" (42:1), so also Christ is God's "Chosen One" (Luke 23:35). And just as the Lord delights in His servant (Isa. 42:1), so also He is well pleased with His Son (Matt. 3:17; Luke 3:22). God promises to put His Spirit on the servant (Isa. 42:1), just as He promised that His Spirit would rest on the Branch (11:1-2), another

name for the Messiah. We are told in 61:1 that God's
Spirit is on the Messiah, and Jesus quoted that verse
and its context in reference to Himself (Luke 4:17-
21). The Lord's servant would bring "justice to the
nations" (Isa. 42:1), a prediction made also of the
Branch in 11:4.

The servant would not "shout or cry out, or raise
his voice" (42:2). Such was true also of the gentle
ministry of Jesus, the "Prince of Peace" (9:6). Far
from breaking a reed already bruised (42:3), the Messiah would heal the sick and "bind up the broken-
hearted" (61:1). Moses had mediated God's law to the
people of Israel, and the Messiah would do the same
for the people of the world (42:4). Moses had been the
first in a long line of prophets to speak in God's name
(Deut. 18:15-20), and Jesus would be the greatest
prophet in that noble tradition (Acts 3:20-23,26).

Matthew 12:15-21 describes one aspect of the
ministry of Jesus, and it does so primarily by quoting
Isaiah 42:1-4, the first of the servant songs. Matthew
saw in Jesus Christ the ultimate fulfillment of
Isaiah's prophecy concerning the servant's call.

THE SERVANT AS PROPHET (Isa. 49:1-6)

The Lord called the servant before he was born
(49:1) and formed him "in the womb" (49:5) to be His
chosen one. The phrases used remind us not only of
the calls of the prophet Jeremiah (Jer. 1:5) and the
apostle Paul (Gal. 1:15) but also cause us to reflect on
the angelic annunciation to the virgin Mary (Luke
1:30-35). The Lord made mention of the name of the
servant from His birth (Isa. 49:1)—the name "that is
above every name" (Phil. 2:9), the name "Jesus,"
because He would "save his people from their sins"
(Matt. 1:21). The mouth of the servant was "like a
sharpened sword" (Isa. 49:1) in the sense that the

Messiah would be an instrument of divine judgment against sinners (Rev. 1:16; 2:12,16).

At first glance, Isaiah 49:3 seems to equate the Lord's servant with the nation of Israel. But 49:5-6 states that the mission of the servant is to bring Israel back to the Lord. Israel personified, the ideal Israel, the Messiah Himself, is therefore once again in view. The Messiah would succeed where national Israel had failed. The Lord would display His splendor in the servant (49:3) by accomplishing a great work of redemption through Him (44:23). Although at first it would appear that the Messiah's ministry had been in vain and without purpose, God would reward Him (49:4) with spiritual offspring (53:10) and divine vindication (1 Tim. 3:16).

The historical background of Isaiah 49:5-6 is the release of the Jews from Babylonian exile in 538 B.C. (see 49:9-12,22), but a greater release from a more sinister captivity is also in view. Together with Genesis 12:1-3 and Exodus 19:5-6, Isaiah 49:6 is sometimes called the "great commission of the Old Testament." In Acts 13:47, Paul and Barnabas quote the last two lines of Isaiah 49:6 in the sense that they share with the Messiah the task of being a "light for the Gentiles" (see also Acts 26:23). Jesus is the light of the world (John 8:12; 9:5; Luke 2:30-32), and He commands His followers to reflect His light (Matt. 5:14-16). Only in such a way will it be possible to bring His "salvation to the ends of the earth" (Isa. 49:6). The great commission mandates a cooperative venture in which Christ and Christians work together to "make disciples of all nations" (Matt. 28:18-20).

THE SERVANT AS MARTYR (Isa. 50:4-9)

"Sovereign LORD" is the only title used by the ser-

vant to refer to God in this song (50:4,5,7,9). It
marks the beginning (50:4) and end (50:9) of the section, and it is used nowhere else in the songs of the
suffering servant. The same Sovereign Lord of the
universe who anoints the Messiah with His Spirit
(61:1) also instructs the servant (50:4). He helps Him
(50:7,9), and He opens His ears to make Him submis-
sive and obedient (50:5; Ps. 40:6). Jesus the Messiah, the Son of God, surrendered to His Father's will
(Matt. 26:39,42,44) and "learned obedience from
what he suffered" (Heb. 5:8).

The Sovereign Lord equipped the servant to sus-
tain the weary (Isa. 50:4; Matt. 11:28) and help the
weak (Isa. 42:3). He wakened the servant's ear (50:4)
and made Him responsive to God's voice. As though
He were a common criminal, the servant was
whipped and flogged (50:6; Matt. 27:26; John 19:1),
mocked and spit upon (Matt. 26:67-68; 27:28-31).

But the ultimate destiny of the servant would be
glory rather than disgrace, honor rather than shame
(Isa. 50:7-8; 49:7; 52:13; 53:10-12). Just as He did
not hide His face from His scornful persecutors
(50:6), so also He set his face "like flint" (50:7), eventually toward Jerusalem (Luke 9:51) where He would
suffer and die. No one could justly bring charges
against Him (Isa. 40:8-9; Matt. 27:23) because He
was sinless (Heb. 4:15). As a garment is eaten up by
moths, so the servant's wicked accusers would be
destroyed (Isa. 50:9)—and the same fate is in store
for all who insult God's people (51:7-8). No one can
justly "bring any charge against those whom God has
chosen" (Rom. 8:33).

THE SERVANT AS SAVIOUR (Isa. 52:13—53:12)

The fourth servant song is the last and longest

and loveliest of them all. In terms of sheer literary beauty it is a pleasure to read and enjoy. The song contains five stanzas of three verses apiece, and each successive stanza is longer than the one preceding it. The fourth servant song, often called the "Gospel in the Old Testament," is quoted more frequently in the New Testament than any other Old Testament passage.

But far more important than its unsurpassed poetic excellence is its profound subject matter. It is the greatest messianic section in the entire Old Testament, providing intimate details about the life, ministry, death, resurrection and glorification of the suffering servant of the Lord seven centuries before the events themselves.

Stanza One: The Divine Servant (52:13-15)

By acting and reigning wisely (52:13; Jer. 23:5), the servant Messiah would insure blessing and prosperity for all His people. Even the wisdom of Solomon was no match for that of Jesus Christ (Luke 11:31). Though He was a servant, God would exalt Him to the highest place of prominence (Isa. 52:13; Phil. 2:5-9) and seat Him at His own right hand (Acts 2:33; Eph. 1:20-23). But first the Messiah would provide "purification for sins" (Heb. 1:3) by sprinkling "many nations" (Isa. 52:15) with His atoning blood, just as the Israelite high priest sprinkled blood on the atonement cover of the Ark of the Covenant once a year for his people's sins (Lev. 16:14-15; 17:11). The servant would undergo inhuman treatment (Isa. 52:14; Psa. 22:6-7; Matt. 27:28-31,39-44) in the course of fulfilling His redemptive mission, the nature of which would eventually be understood by kings (Isa. 52:15) and commoners (Rom. 15:20-21) alike.

Stanza Two: The Divine Sufferer (53:1-3)

Isaiah 53 is the middle and key chapter in Isaiah 40–66 as well as in 49–57, the subject of which is the doctrine of salvation. Polycarp, the second-century bishop of Smyrna in Asia Minor, perhaps the last survivor of those who had talked with the eyewitnesses of Jesus, and himself martyred for his faith, called Isaiah 53 the "golden passion of the Old Testament." It is surely the best-known and best-loved chapter in Isaiah.

The "message" of 53:1 is the good news about salvation, given by the prophet (28:9) to Jerusalem (52:7) and the nations (52:10) and, ultimately, to all mankind through Christ (John 12:37-38; Rom. 10:16-17). The message concerned the "root" (Isa. 53:2; 11:10), the "Branch" (4:2; 11:1; Zech. 3:8), the tender "shoot" (Isa. 53:2; 11:1), whose humble beginnings would take their rise from the demoralized dynasty of David, the "stump of Jesse" (11:1). In the final week of His suffering, Jesus possessed anything but regal bearing. He had "no beauty or majesty" (53:2; Luke 18:31-32). He was despised and treated with contempt (Isa. 53:3; Ps. 22:6), esteemed by no one, and "rejected" (Isa. 53:3) even by His own people (John 1:10-11). It can indeed be said of Christ that He was "familiar with suffering."

Stanza Three: The Divine Substitute (53:4-6)

" . . . our . . . our [53:4] . . . our . . . our . . . us . . . we [53:5] . . . We . . . us . . . us" (53:6): No less than nine times in these three verses we are told that someone else bore our sicknesses and sorrows, that someone else died for our sins, that someone else substituted His life for ours. Although people thought that God was causing the servant to suffer for His own sins (53:4), such was not the case. Disease often results from dissolute living and is ultimately a consequence of our sinful nature, so the intimate connection between sickness and sin is drawn in 53:4-5. It was Jesus who "took up our infirmities and carried our sorrows," as Matthew 8:16-17 points out. It was Jesus who was "pierced for our transgressions," a fact understood by evangelist (John 19:34) and apostle (Rom. 4:25) alike. And "by his wounds"—the wounds of Jesus—we have been healed (1 Pet. 2:24), we have been forgiven.

All of this has happened despite our straying and waywardness (Isa. 53:6), as 1 Peter 2:24-25 also asserts. Prodigal sons and daughters of every age can return to the Father because of what Jesus has done. The Lord has laid on Jesus "the iniquity of us all" (Isa. 53:6), just as the Israelite priest laid his hands on the scapegoat and symbolically put his people's sins on it (Lev. 16:21). Christ "bore our sins in his body on the tree" (1 Pet. 2:24).

Stanza Four: The Divine Sacrifice (53:7-9)

"Led like a lamb to the slaughter" (53:7), the servant—the "Lamb of God" (John 1:29,35)—went willingly to his death (Rev. 5:6). Philip explained to an Ethiopian eunuch that the lamb of Isaiah 53:7-8 was not the prophet Isaiah but was Jesus Christ (Acts 8:26-35). The One who was "oppressed and afflicted" and yet "did not open his mouth" (Isa. 53:7) is Jesus, who remained silent in the presence of His accusers (Matt. 27:12-14; Mark 14:60-61; 15:4-5; Luke 23:8-9; John 19:8-9). His trial was unfair and His death sentence endangered His progeny (Isa. 53:8), but His spiritual "offspring" (53:10) would carry on His redemptive ministry. The suffering servant was "assigned a grave with the wicked, and with the rich in his death" (53:9), dying on a cross between two robbers (Matt. 27:38; Mark 15:27; Luke 23:32) and being given an honorable burial in a new tomb owned by the wealthy Joseph of Arimathea (Matt. 27:57-60; Mark 15:43-46; Luke 23:50-53; John 19:38-42). In suffering voluntarily for us, Jesus gave us an example of courage and a lesson in faithfulness—a lesson highlighted by the apostle Peter, who in 1 Peter 2:21-23 quotes the last two lines of Isaiah 53:9.

Stanza Five: The Divine Satisfaction (53:10-12)

The suffering and death of the servant would be followed by resurrection, and He would then be satisfied (53:11)—not because He was alive again, but because His death and resurrection had secured the justification of sinful mankind (53:11; Rom. 4:25). It was God's will that Jesus should suffer and die (53:10; Acts 2:23), because only the sinless can die for the sinful (1 Pet. 1:18-20). The death of Christ is compared to a "guilt offering" (Isa. 53:10), a sacrifice that required the death of an unblemished animal (Lev. 5:15) for sins intentional (6:1) and unintentional (5:18).

Death could not keep its prey, however, and Jesus rose from the grave. In so doing He prolonged His days (Isa. 53:10) as the eternal Lord (9:6) who lives forever (Heb. 13:8; Rev. 22:13). The two oldest known scrolls of the book of Isaiah, found in 1947 in a cave near the northwest shore of the Dead Sea, both display the word *light* as the object of the verb *see* in 53:11. In triumph Jesus emerged from the darkness of death and saw the light of resurrection life, making it possible for Paul to declare that Christ was raised "according to the Scriptures" (1 Cor. 15:4). The final reference to the servant of the Lord in Isaiah is the only case in which the word *servant* is qualified by an adjective. Jesus is God's "righteous servant"

(53:11) in the sense that His resurrection vindicates His sinless righteousness. And because Christ is righteous, He justified "many" when He bore their iniquities (53:11; Rom. 5:18-19).

Jesus "poured out his life unto death" (Isa. 53:11), "even death on a cross" (Phil. 2:8). A great victory has thus been won (Phil. 2:9-11), symbolized by dividing the spoils of battle (Isa. 53:12). Jesus was "numbered with the transgressors" (53:12), an historical event that took place nearly two thousand years ago (Luke 22:37) and was predicted by Isaiah seven centuries earlier. But the resurrected Christ is our living Lord, who intercedes for "those who come to God through him" (Heb. 7:25)—an intercessory ministry whose initial stages were also predicted in Isa. 53:12.

SERVANT AND SERVANTS

After Isaiah 53, the singular word *servant* never appears again in the book of Isaiah. The pyramid or cone diagram of the suffering servant of the Lord reaches its apex in 53:11, and from this point on every occurrence of the word *servant* in Isaiah is in the plural—"servants" (54:17; 63:17; 65:8-9,13-15; 66:14)—referring to Jewish and Gentile believers who are the faithful "offspring" (53:10) of Isaiah's servant. The diagram of the cone becomes a drawing of an hourglass, because just as the development of the "servant" (singular) concept in Isaiah became more and more constricted as it began with the entire nation of Israel, narrowed to remnant Israel, and peaked in the Messiah, so also the development of the "servants" (plural) concept in the New Testament becomes more and more expanded as it begins with Christ, grows into a persecuted Christian fellowship, and continues to enlarge down to the present day.

The cone of Israel has become the hourglass of the Church.

This means that we are truly members of the Church only as we are truly servants. Belief in Christ involves suffering for Him (Phil. 1:29). He took the form of a servant (2:7), and our attitude concerning servanthood should be the same as His (2:5). Like Paul, we should want to know not only "Christ and the power of His resurrection" but also the "fellowship of sharing in his sufferings" (3:10). To follow Him faithfully into the valley of suffering means that some day we will also "share in his glory" (Rom. 8:17).

Frank E. Gaebelein, the founding headmaster of the Stony Brook School on Long Island in New York, was a scholar, preacher, author, editor, concert pianist, and Alpine mountaineer. His competence in everything he undertook was immediately recognized by all who knew him. He was one of the truly great Christian statesmen of our time. But Gaebelein's greatness did not reside in his accomplishments or abilities, however formidable one might consider them. He was a great man because of his profound faith in Christ and because of his genuine concern for the needs of God's people around the world. He was a great man not because he was a leader but because he was a servant. That is why Karl E. Soderstrom, current headmaster of Stony Brook, began and ended his message at the memorial service following Frank Gaebelein's death in January, 1983, with Jesus' call to greatness as recorded in Mark 10:43: "Whoever wants to become great among you must be your servant."

For Study or Discussion

1. Who is "the servant" in Isaiah?

2. What New Testament references support the idea that "the servant" was Jesus?

3. Did Jesus ever "shout or cry out, or raise his voice?" If so, who was Isaiah 42:2 referring to?

4. Why is Isaiah 53 sometimes called the "Calvary chapter?"

5. What is meant by "the divine substitute"?

6. Explain the meaning of "guilt offering" in 53:10.

13

ISAIAH'S MESSIAH

Isaiah 58—66

We have now come to the last nine chapters of Isaiah, the third and final section of the Book of Consolation. After reading and pondering the magnificent passages concerning the suffering servant of the Lord in the two earlier sections, it might seem somewhat anticlimactic to consider other themes. But the servant who came to earth the first time almost two thousand years ago will come again, as the Scriptures so clearly teach. His second coming is one of the topics treated in Isaiah 58—66, a section that stresses eschatology, the doctrine of the last days.

DENUNCIATION OF ISRAEL'S SINS (Isa. 58—59)

The final section of Isaiah begins as the first section did: The Lord calls Israel to account because of their rebellion against Him (58:1; 1:2). Isaiah's countrymen were no more righteous in the days of his later ministry than they had been during his earlier years. At that time the Lord had not been pleased with the multitude of their sacrifices (1:11), and the fact that they now seek Him out day after day does not impress Him either (58:2). God abhors hypocrisy in every age (29:13-14).

The people of Judah, whether Isaiah's contemporaries or their descendants in Babylonian exile, are guilty of fasting in a way that is unacceptable to God (58:3-12). They thought that all they had to do while fasting was to humble themselves (58:3) and put on the clothes of mourning (58:5). But, as Jesus taught, such fasting is sheer hypocrisy (Matt. 6:16-18) and God will not honor it. Often it is accompanied by exploitation (Isa. 58:3), by quarreling (58:4), by oppression (58:6), by gossip (58:9). True fasting, however, has a spiritual dimension that is more important than the physical ritual itself. During the siege of Jerusalem just before 586 B.C. her citizens released their Hebrew slaves, only to change their minds and enslave them again (Jer. 34:8-11). By contrast, true fasting includes setting the oppressed free and breaking every yoke (Isa. 58:6). It involves providing food for the hungry, shelter for the wanderer, and clothing for the naked (58:7), as Jesus also reminded us (Matt. 25:36-40). Such deeds of kindness and mercy demonstrate the kind of heart attitude that the Lord honors. He hears us when we obey Him (Isa. 58:9), but we cannot expect Him to listen to us when we are disobedient (58:4; 59:2). God's people exiled in Babylon had to learn that their own needs would be met (58:11) only if they were genuinely concerned about the needs of others (58:10). Following their release from captivity their descendants would then be able to repair Jerusalem's broken walls (58:12) under the leadership of Nehemiah (Neh. 2:17). But the Lord's people are often slow to learn: The first group of exiles who returned to Jerusalem had to be warned by God that they had not been fasting in the proper way (Zech. 7:5).

Just as God's chosen people are not to do simply

as they please on their days of fasting (Isa. 58:3), so also they are not to do as they please on the Sabbath (58:13). The Lord will bless them only if they honor Him by honoring His holy day (58:14; Jer. 17:21-27).

To the specific examples of improper fasting and improper Sabbath observance is added a catalogue of other sins (Isa. 59:1-15a). They center around the deplorable lack of justice and righteousness in business dealings and interpersonal relationships (59:4,8,9,11,14). The three most common Old Testament terms for wickedness describe the evil deeds of the people of Judah (59:12): "sins," referring to missing the target of righteousness that God has set up; "offenses," a description of persistent rebellion against His sovereignty; and "iniquities," a series of premeditated perversions of His holy will. Such attitudes and activities always separate us from our God (59:2; Jer. 5:25) and make it impossible for Him to hear our prayers (Isa. 59:1-2; 58:4). Murder (59:3), lying (59:4), violence (59:6), treachery (59:13), dishonesty (59:14)—the list goes on and on. Paul's discussion of the universal and pervasive nature of sin in Romans 3 quotes several lines from Isaiah 59:7-8, testifying to the importance of Isaiah 59 for a proper understanding of what sin really means (Rom. 3:15-17). And Isaiah 59:7 may itself be a quotation from an earlier source (Prov. 1:16).

Sins so flagrant always bring divine displeasure and judgment (Isa. 59:15b-19). No one can help God in His task of retribution (59:16; 63:5). As the believer requires spiritual armor in his battle against the devil (Eph. 6:11-17), so the Lord figuratively puts on spiritual garments (Isa. 59:17) as He prepares to punish all who have sinned against Him, whether His chosen people or the nations of the world (Isa. 59:18-19).

The remnant who repent, however, would not be judged (59:20-21). The Redeemer would accompany the exiles to Jerusalem, to be sure, but the greater fulfillment of 59:20-21 would take place in the distant future at the second coming of Christ, as Paul correctly recognized (Rom. 11:26-27). The Lord's covenant of Isaiah 59:21 is the new covenant of Jeremiah 31:31-34, fulfilled ultimately in Jesus (Heb. 9:15). No longer written merely on tablets of stone, the words of the Lord would be written on the hearts (Jer. 31:33) and spoken by the mouths of His people forever (Isa. 59:21).

THE COMING MESSIANIC AGE (Isa. 60—62)

Zion's Future Glory (Chap 60)

A careful reading of Matthew 24 leads to the conclusion that its verses interweave predictions of the destruction of Jerusalem in A.D. 70 (the near future) with predictions of the second coming of Christ (the remote future). Similarly, a careful reading of Isaiah 60 leads to the conclusion that its verses interweave predictions of the return of the exiled Jews to Jerusalem in 538 B.C. (the relatively near future) with predictions concerning the new Jerusalem of the last days (the remote future).

Isaiah 60:4, like 49:18,22, rejoices in the coming return of Jerusalem's sons and daughters from captivity. The contribution of the Persian king Darius to the Temple (Ezra 6:8-9) may be a partial fulfillment of the prophecy that the wealth of the nations would come to Zion (Isa. 60:5). Midian, Ephah, Sheba, Kedar, and Nebaioth—all descendants of Abraham (Gen. 25:2-4,13)—would bring their riches to the city and Temple (Isa. 60:6-7). As the queen of Sheba had brought gold and spices to Solomon, the builder of the first Temple (1 Kings 10:2), so gold and incense would come from Sheba to Jerusalem to adorn the second Temple (Isa. 60:6). As the ships of Tarshish had brought silver and gold to Solomon (1 Kings 10:22), so they would carry silver and gold to honor the Lord (Isa. 60:9) in the context of the rebuilding of the walls of Jerusalem (60:10) as mandated by the decree of the Persian king Artaxerxes in 445 B.C. (Neh. 2:8). As cedars of Lebanon, along with pine trees, were used in the construction of Solomon's Temple (1 Kings 5:10,18), so these and other kinds of wood would adorn the second Temple (Isa. 60:13). And just as gold and silver were plentiful in the days of Solomon (1 Kings 10:21,27), so also they would be plentiful in the Jerusalem yet to be restored (Isa. 60:17).

But Isaiah's description of the physical city of the relatively near future blends effortlessly into the glorious Zion known as the new Jerusalem. In that far more distant future, the dwelling place of the faithful will have God Himself as their light (60:1-3), their "everlasting light" (60:19-20; Rev. 21:23; 22:5). The gates of the new Jerusalem will always be open (Isa. 60:11; Rev. 21:25). The future Zion will be called "The City of the LORD" (Isa. 60:14), a title similar to that used in Hebrews 12:22 ("the city of the living God"). In the new Jerusalem, sorrow will be no more (Isa. 60:20; Rev. 21:4). Only the redeemed will live there (Isa. 60:21; Rev. 21:27).

In Matthew 24 it is not always easy to tell when the author is referring to the near future and when he is talking about the remote future, and the same is true in Isaiah 60. In some verses the description could fit either situation, and in a few verses both the near and remote time frames may be intended (the former prefiguring the latter). The message of Isaiah 60, in any event, is that Zion's future in history and beyond history will be more glorious than its past.

The Messiah's Future Ministry (Chap. 61)

In the synagogue at Nazareth, early in His ministry, Jesus read aloud most of Isaiah 61:1-2 (Luke 4:16-19) and then said to the people seated before Him, "Today this scripture is fulfilled in your hearing" (Luke 4:21). "The Spirit of the Sovereign Lord" (Isa. 61:1) was on Jesus Christ (11:2; 42:1; Luke 3:22). The Hebrew verb for "anointed" (Isa. 61:1) is the origin of our word *Messiah,* and the word *Christ* comes from a Greek verb meaning "anointed" (John 1:41; 4:25). One aspect of Jesus' mission was to "preach good news to the poor" (Isa. 61:1; Matt. 11:5; Luke 7:22). His healing and redemptive ministry, sketched in the last three lines of Isaiah 61:1, is prefigured in a limited sense in the release of the Jewish exiles from Babylon (as also in 42:7). But although Isaiah's captive countrymen may have served as his model, the eyes of the inspired prophet looked far into the future as he summarized the Messiah's lifework: "to proclaim the year of the Lord's favor" (61:2).

And Jesus Himself summarized it in the same words. In the synagogue at Nazareth He stopped His oral reading after the word "favor" (Luke 4:19-20) because the next clause—"the day of vengeance of our God" (Isa. 61:2)—describes an event that will not occur until Jesus' second coming. His earthly ministry, however, would include a message of comfort for all who mourn (61:2-3), as He proclaimed in His sermon on the mount (Matt. 5:4).

After Isaiah 61:3, the prophet's vision returns to the time of the Babylonian exile (61:4-11). Following their release the Jews would rebuild Jerusalem and the other cities and towns of Judah (61:4). They would resume their vocation as a "kingdom of priests" (Exod. 19:6) to the nations around them (Isa. 61:6). Israel, the Lord's "firstborn son" (Exod. 4:22), would "receive a double portion" of God's blessings (Isa. 61:7) as the rightful heir of His promises (Zech. 9:12; see Deut. 21:17) and to correspond to the double punishment the people had "received" during their years of exile (Isa. 40:2). Their Babylonian conquerors had oppressed and exploited them, but the Lord in His faithfulness (not theirs) would make an everlasting covenant with them (61:8) and bless them once again with the promises originally given to Abraham (61:9; Gen. 12:1-3). Zion responds to God's goodness with a song of gratitude and praise in Isaiah 61:10-11.

Jerusalem's Future Relationship (Chap. 62)

In 62:1-7, Isaiah speaks on behalf of the Lord. Jerusalem and her citizens would receive a new name, given to them by the Lord (62:2) and signifying a restored relationship. The city would no longer be called "Deserted" (62:4,12) but would be called *Hephzibah* (Hebrew for "my delight is in her")—the name also of the wife of King Hezekiah (2 Kings 21:1), during whose reign Isaiah spent the latter years of his ministry. Jerusalem's land would no longer be called "Desolate" (Isa. 62:4) but would be called *Beulah* (Hebrew for "married"), because the Lord Himself would again seek after His people (62:12) and become their husband (Hos. 2:16). The Hebrew word translated "sons" in Isaiah 62:5 can also be translated as "builder," referring to the God who would marry Jerusalem and build her up by bringing back her captive exiles (Ps. 147:2). The prophet expresses his eagerness for the coming of that happy day (Isa. 62:6-7), and the Lord responds by promising that Jerusalem's future resources would be used by her citizens rather than her enemies (62:8-9). The call then rings out for the Jews to leave the city of Babylon through her gates and to get ready to march to Jerusalem along the highway prepared for them (62:10).

Once again the prophet's vision leaps to the distant future as he foresees the coming of the Saviour, not only of Jerusalem but also of the entire world. Although 62:11 may refer initially to Jesus' triumphal entry into Jerusalem on Palm Sunday (Zech. 9:9; Matt. 21:5), Revelation 22:12 indicates that ultimately it points forward to the second coming of Christ. Only then will all who trust the Lord be truly "The Holy People, the Redeemed" (Isa. 62:12).

JUDGMENT AND SALVATION (Isa. 63—66)

The last four chapters of Isaiah present a series of oracles that alternate between the twin themes of doom and redemption and generally tend to treat the historical manifestations of those themes in chronological order.

Past (63:1-14)

Esau, the hostile brother of Jacob (Gen. 27:41; Obad. 8–10), was the ancestor of the Edomites, the agelong enemies of Jacob's Israelite descendants. But Edom also symbolized a world at enmity with God and His people (Isa. 63:1-6; 34:5-15). Wine, the "blood of grapes" (Gen. 49:11), is used figuratively to represent the fury that fills the cup of God's wrath in the last days (Rev. 16:19), and "treading the winepress" is a symbol of judgment not only in Isaiah 63:2-3 but also in Revelation 14:17-20; 19:13-16. Nevertheless, although the ultimate fulfillment of Isaiah 63:1-6 may relate to the final battle at Christ's second coming (compare especially 63:1 with Rev. 19:13), the primary reference would seem to be the Lord's past victories over Edom (63:1-3) and the nations symbolized by her (63:6).

In response to the Lord's military triumphs, Isaiah sings a hymn of praise in which he recalls the mighty acts of God in the past (63:7-14): dividing the waters of the Red Sea (63:11-13), leading His people through the desert with the angel of His presence (63:9), putting His Spirit on Moses and seventy elders (63:11; Num. 11:17,25), and bringing the people into the land of Canaan (Isa. 63:14). But all did not go smoothly, because they rebelled against the Lord (63:10)—not only in the desert (Num. 20:10) but also during the long centuries they spent settling down in Canaan (Neh. 9:26-30).

Present (63:15—65:16)

Isaiah, knowing that the rebellion of God's people in the past continues to the present (1:2; 59:12-13), offers a prayer of lamentation and confession and asks for a renewal of God's covenant love (63:15—64:12). He pleads with the Lord to look down from heaven (63:15), to "rend the heavens and come down" (64:1) as He had done at Mount Sinai (64:3; Exod. 19:18). Although Judah's human fathers might abandon them (Isa. 63:16), Isaiah prays that their heavenly Father would continue His creative and redemptive work in their midst (63:16; 64:8). The prophet makes a distinction (63:19) between God's "servants" (63:17) and their "enemies" (63:18), the Babylonians, who destroyed Solomon's Temple in 586 B.C. (64:11; Ps. 74:3-7). He wants the Lord to vindicate His honor in the world (Isa. 64:2). God's unique being and activity are described in terms (64:4) that the apostle Paul found useful (1 Cor. 2:9) to characterize spiritual truth revealed by God alone. It is that kind of truth that Isaiah seeks for himself and his countrymen (Isa. 64:5), but he knows full well that the Lord remains a hidden God to those who sin against Him and refuse to repent (64:7). He therefore confesses the sins of Judah, comparing even their righteous acts to the ceremonially unclean pieces of cloth used by a woman during her monthly period (64:6; Lev. 15:19-24; Ezek. 36:17). He earnestly prays that God will not reject His people or remember their sins forever (Isa. 64:9,12).

Isaiah's loving Lord answers his Servant (65:1-16), but in judgment as well as in mercy. The nation (65:1), the obstinate people (65:2-3) who continually provoked Him, would be judged (65:7). But the Lord's servants (65:8-9,13-15), the believing remnant, would be blessed (65:8). In Romans 10:20, Paul quotes part of Isaiah 65:1 to demonstrate the fact that God often takes the initiative in getting His message across even to people who may not want to hear it—people like those of Isaiah's day who were pursuing such pagan practices as eating pig's flesh and sacrificing pig's blood (65:4; 66:3,17; Lev. 11:7-8), burning incense to other deities (Isa. 65:3; Jer. 44:17-19), and bringing offerings to personified gods of good luck and sinister fate (Isa. 65:11). The Lord wants to help such people (65:2), as Paul clearly understood (Rom. 10:21). But they often ignore God and refuse to listen to His pleading voice (Isa. 65:11-12).

The Lord's people, however, would be blessed by Him (65:13-16). From the pastures of Sharon in the west to the Valley of Achor in the east (65:10), from Jacob in the north to Judah in the south (65:9), the Lord's servants would possess His mountains and inherit His land. They would eat and drink, they would rejoice and sing (65:13-14). God would give them another name (65:15), a new name (62:2), and prove Himself to be true to His promises (65:16; 2 Cor. 1:20).

Future (65:17—66:24)

The relatively near future is in view to some extent (for example 65:21-23; 66:3-11,17-21), but Isaiah's prophetic vision is more specifically concerned with a more remote future. The new heavens and the new earth (65:17; 66:22; 2 Pet. 3:13) are connected by Revelation 21:1-2 with the new Jerusalem, which God will some day create to be a delight (Isa. 65:18). The "former things" (65:17), the "old order of things" (Rev. 21:4), will never again come to mind. In the New Jerusalem there will be no more weeping or crying (Isa. 65:19; Rev. 21:4), and in the Messiah's kingdom nature itself will be redeemed (Isa. 65:25; 11:6-9). The Sovereign Lord, who does not live in houses made by men (66:1-2; Acts 7:48-50), will accomplish all these things.

But the future, like the present and the past, includes judgment as well as salvation (Isa. 66:14-16). Part of the last verse of Isaiah is quoted in Mark 9:48, where the context describes the horrors of hell. Part of the last verse of Isaiah mentions fire unquenchable, an aspect of judgment referred to also in Matthew 3:12. And part of the last verse of Isaiah is linked to the beginning of Isaiah's message in 1:2: Both passages underscore the irony of human rebellion against divine love.

THEMES FROM ISAIAH 58—66

It would be unfair to Isaiah, however, to leave the impression that the book as a whole is negative in its thrust. Isaiah's name means "The LORD Saves," and salvation is the primary topic treated in his book (45:22). In an attempt to summarize the message of Isaiah 58—66 and that of the whole book as well, three characteristics of Isaiah's God stand out.

God is good. He delights in blessing His faithful people (58:13-14; 62:4-5), and He promises them strength for today and hope for tomorrow (61:3-7). His Messiah preaches good news to the poor (61:1), and He Himself does "many good things" for His followers (63:7). To one and all He sends out this proclamation: "Listen, listen to me, and eat what is good, and your soul will delight in the richest of fare" (55:2). The goodness of God has no equal in heaven or on earth.

God is great. He is strong and mighty, and He needs no help no matter what He does (59:16; 63:5). In redemption, He is "mighty to save" (63:1); in judgment, He comes "like a pent-up flood" (59:19). In order to instruct His people in the way that they should walk, He made His law "great and glorious" (42:21). He accomplishes everything, in heaven and on earth, by means of "his great power and mighty strength" (40:26). "Great is the Holy One of Israel among you" (12:6).

God is gracious. The Lord's goodness and greatness are not mere abstractions. He uses them to benefit those who are in need, because He is a God of mercy and compassion. His mercy is expressed in His redemptive love (63:9); His compassion is directed toward His chosen people (63:7). Although in righteous anger He judges sin, in gracious favor He shows compassion (60:10). He longs to be gracious to us (30:18); He promises to be gracious when we cry for help (30:19). Let us therefore pray with the prophet Isaiah: "O LORD, be gracious to us; we long for you. Be our strength every morning, our salvation in time of distress" (33:2).

Isaiah's God—and ours—is good, and great, and gracious.

For Study or Discussion

1. What is the "new Jerusalem"?

2. How did God's standards of social justice change from the time of Isaiah to the time of James (Isaiah 58; James 5)?

3. What event is referred to in Isaiah 62:11?

4. What is the "new name" of the Lord's servants? (Isaiah 62:2; 65:15)

5. What is the "sign" of Isaiah 66:19?

BIBLIOGRAPHY

(Inclusion of a book in the following list does not necessarily indicate wholesale approval of the author's viewpoint or methodology.)

Alexander, Joseph Addison. *The Earlier Prophecies of Isaiah.* New York: Wiley and Putnam, 1846.

Archer, Gleason L., Jr. "Isaiah." In Charles F. Pfeiffer and Everett F. Harrison, eds., *The Wycliffe Bible Commentary.* Chicago: Moody Press, 1962, pp. 605-654.

Culver, Robert D. *The Sufferings and the Glory of the Lord's Righteous Servant.* Moline, Illinois: Christian Service Foundation, 1958.

Delitzsch, Franz. *Biblical Commentary on the Prophecies of Isaiah.* 2 vols. Grand Rapids, Michigan: William B. Eerdmans Publishing Company, 1954 (1877).

Keith, Alexander. *Isaiah as It Is: Or, Judah and Jerusalem the Subjects of Isaiah's Prophesying.* Edinburgh: William Whyte and Company, 1850.

Kidner, Derek. "Isaiah." In D. Guthrie, J. A. Motyer, A. M. Stibbs and D. J. Wiseman, eds., *The New Bible Commentary: Revised.* Grand Rapids,

Michigan: William B. Eerdmans Publishing Company, 1970, pp. 588-625.

Leupold, H. C. *Exposition of Isaiah.* 2 vols. Grand Rapids, Michigan: Baker Book House, 1968.

MacRae, Allan A. *The Gospel of Isaiah.* Chicago: Moody Press, 1977.

Payne, David F. "Isaiah." In G. C. D. Howley, F. F. Bruce and H. L. Ellison, eds., *The New Layman's Bible Commentary.* Grand Rapids, Michigan: Zondervan Publishing House, 1979, pp. 763-814.

Pieper, August. *Isaiah II.* Milwaukee: Northwestern Publishing House, 1979.

Robinson, George L. *The Book of Isaiah.* Grand Rapids, Michigan: Baker Book House, 1954.

Smith, George Adam. *The Book of Isaiah.* 2 vols. New York: Harper and Brothers Publishers, 1927.

Young, Edward J. *The Book of Isaiah.* 3 vols. Grand Rapids, Michigan: William B. Eerdmans Publishing Company, 1965, 1969, 1972.